Red House to Exodus

Growing up in Harpenden in the 1950s and 1960s

BY THE SAME AUTHOR

Grandma's Poetry Book (2014) – a collection documenting the first thirteen years of grand-parenting. The first-time grandmother's often wobbly journey.

Should I Wear Floral and other poems on Life, Love and Leaving, a celebration of the last 25 years (2017)

She tweets @Dinahcas
Is on Facebook as Di Castle – Writer
https://wordpress.com/view/dicastlewriter.wordpress.com

Her blogs can be read on websites She reviews books here
https://wordpress.com/view/disbookblog.wordpress.com

Her mental health blog www.dismindmatters.wordpress.com has been widely read and enjoyed by both those struggling with depression and anxiety and others who care for them.

Her first blog was http://dicastle32.blogspot.com/

Red House to Exodus

Growing up in Harpenden in the 1950s and 1960s

Di Castle

Copyright © 2024 Di Castle

The moral right of the author has been asserted.

Apart from any fair dealing for the purposes of research or private study, or criticism or review, as permitted under the Copyright, Designs and Patents Act 1988, this publication may only be reproduced, stored or transmitted, in any form or by any means, with the prior permission in writing of the publishers, or in the case of reprographic reproduction in accordance with the terms of licences issued by the Copyright Licensing Agency. Enquiries concerning reproduction outside those terms should be sent to the publishers.

Troubador Publishing Ltd
Unit E2 Airfield Business Park
Harrison Road, Market Harborough
Leicestershire LE16 7UL
Tel: 0116 279 2299
Email: books@troubador.co.uk
Web: www.troubador.co.uk

ISBN 978-1-83628-026-2

British Library Cataloguing in Publication Data.
A catalogue record for this book is available from the British Library.

Printed and bound in Great Britain by 4edge Limited
Typeset in 11pt Minion Pro by Troubador Publishing Ltd, Leicester, UK

For Amy, Erin, James, Tom, Sam, Eva and Rita – your world is far different to the one in which I grew up. If you have half the fun, love and happy experiences I have enjoyed in life, you will be rich indeed.

Also in memory of my dear school friend, Gill, who is mentioned several times but sadly passed away before the book was finished.

'I love how you share the history – it's so personal (albeit from before you were born) and engaging.'
Helen Baggott, editor

Notes from the Author

Some names have been changed other than close family members who have passed on.

This book should appeal to people in Harpenden but will also be of interest to anyone born in the post-war period as national and international landmarks are mentioned. There are already some memoirs set in Harpenden but most authors grew up in more affluent parts of the village and went to private school whereas I grew up in South Harpenden (known as the Bowling Alley) and was educated in the state system.

I like to combine humour and historical research either of the time or the area. I have used a younger voice in the early part of the book and later this voice is more mature.

Introduction

Why write an autobiography? I'm gardening and am often amazed at the tricks learnt from my dad. Crafting a memoir ensures we dig deep, the process triggering more recollections. Reminiscences of encounters, experiences and feelings tingle at the fingertips. If we do not put pen to paper in the autumn of our life, there will be a day when we cannot remember. Once in print, a memoir can be read by others and considerable joy may result.

When I contacted some of my peers about life in the 1950s one reply said 'are you talking about the 'Janet and John' world which we all inhabited, when – for better or for worse – no-one was divorced, unemployed, black or, as some used to say when in London, coloured. You go to church each Sunday, on holiday with relatives at the English seaside, you *Listen with Mother* or to late-afternoon radio programmes and *The Archers*, and everything is safe and secure …?' well not exactly.

Politicians, celebrities and other persons of renown have always written memoirs, many using ghost writers. At the time of writing, the 'misery memoir' which had permeated the publishing world, with creative expression used as a cathartic force on unhappy childhood memories was thankfully less popular. Certainly, this genre is not the case here, as I grew up happily during the post-war period, an era of constant fascination.

This memoir has been sixteen years in the making, with distractions including writing two poetry books, a few novels, taking holidays, moving house and enjoying grandchildren. Procrastination sees me in my eighth decade with little time left to write all the stories bubbling in my brain. Oh the folly of youth. Believing we are invincible, immortal, we are quick to interrupt, slow to listen and fail to ask pertinent questions. My time has been put to good use, raising children and thirty-five years teaching three generations life and work skills: such experience is a writer's material.

Our past, oral history and family stories die with our parents and mine wrote nothing down, barely labelling their photo albums, but I am grateful to them for one important gift. They talked at length about their childhoods, young married life, Harpenden history and our relatives.

Fast forward and with the arrival of grandchildren I recognised the value of leaving a legacy – a family history, its context being the fast developing post-war years.

So what was life like in 1945? Well, there were no computers like the one I am using, no washing machines, microwaves or television and only a limited choice of radio programmes broadcast via wireless radios the size of a modern drinks cabinet. Few had telephones and only the rich owned cars, cranking them into life with a starting handle at the front. Most people cycled, walked or used buses. There were cinemas with black and white films but no special effects. Talking movies were appearing in cinemas but Pathé News was the only 'moving' visual representation of wartime events and post-war life in Britain. Music in the home was via piano or other instruments and could be reproduced on Bakelite records on wind-up gramophones.

Standards of living were immeasurably lower at the end of the Second World War. Most people lived at home with parents or rented their homes. The country's finances had been tied up in the war effort and there was no financial backing for homes – although, following the bombing of our cities, a building programme was well under way. Household consumption was restricted by rationing. The allocated measure of sweets and biscuits was bought loose rather than in packets and sold by weight, given out in paper bags.

I had written stories since I could hold a pen but the 'lightbulb moment' was in October 2002 when two friends from school made contact via the website Friends Reunited. One expressed surprised I hadn't been seen in print. She had been a fan when I read my creations at the back of the French class.

Around the same time, I attended a local writers' group meeting in Swanage where a fellow writer read an autobiographical account of her schooldays – which, she said, she was compiling for her grandchildren. Their life, as she said, was different to hers in the 1930s. It was an amusing and heart-warming account which reignited some of my own school memories. I thought it commendable – the idea of leaving one's life history to grandchildren. It is, after all, their heritage. Suitably inspired, I bought a large red journal and entered what I could remember as it came to me over a period of three or four years. It was a non-chronological anecdotal account. In 2007 I began researching family history and collected more anecdotes. I also began research about Harpenden, bought books on the 1800s and scrutinised family photographs closely, visiting the quarterly Exhibitions of the Harpenden Local History Society. I wrote to the *Herts Advertiser* asking people to contact me – with considerable response. On one visit, I obtained a few books about Harpenden between the two world wars. The books lacked any detailed reference to South Harpenden, the Bowling Alley and Southdown which I have sought to address in this memoir.

This book therefore relates a 1950s Harpenden childhood and, as such, I hope it appeals to many readers – not just those who live or have lived in the town.

1951

'I need to have a talk with you.' Oh no. The horror must show on my face. This is ominous. When my mother says this it's a sign I am in trouble.

From behind her back she brings into view a rather battered exercise book with some cartoon caricatures drawn over the front cover.

'It's your book.' This wasn't really how I anticipated getting published.

'Yes.' I mustn't sound sulky but there's obviously something wrong with it. I sit and wait. Perhaps she likes it. I think it's really funny.

Mum turns the book round to remind me of the title, My Life Story.

'It's just … you've written about very private things in here.'

Of course, I think. What did she expect?

'It's just, hmm, well if anyone else reads it, like hmm the neighbours … I don't know what they would think …'

So what's to do with it? I don't even need to ask. The pages are being ripped out. How can a mother do this?

This is unbelievable. I think my writing captures the humorous essence of the daily happenings in our household. There's my dad shaving in the sink and farting, myself being told that, as a toddler I'd mess my pants halfway down the garden path and all the snippets of life in Grove Avenue overheard at Sunday dinner. There's our neighbour Mrs … Oh no. That page is a goner too. And as for that funny piece about Mrs Whatshername being seen in the long grass with Mr you-know who.

Ooops. That's censored too.

I haven't been writing long. Really, it's only since I learnt to put letters together. Now I've learnt how words go together in a way people love to read. After all, I'm only six. Surely people want to read about funny things?

No?

I sigh. It's clear my talent isn't appreciated. My friend's mother suggested Mum send my writing to a magazine but now I'm not so sure.

'That bit about picking out my false teeth.' Dad's eyes are twinkling.

'Enough!' Mum has spoken and that's all there is to it.

Weston's Grocery, Southdown Road, South Harpenden, May 1950

'I am sorry, I don't have any.'

Oh no, my mother is telling a fib!

There's silence and an air of disappointment on the woman's face.

I'm sitting on the counter singing and dangling my legs, the smell of broken biscuits tickling my nose. I slide back and forth on the dark brown highly-polished wooden surface. Seconds pass but it seems like minutes.

'She has really. She's got loads under the counter!'

A gasp hits the air like a boxer's punch. My mother's face turns scarlet in tune with her hair and she shuffles her feet with discomfort. Her head shakes as the customer raises her eyebrows.

I bet the woman wishes she'd never asked for sugar.

Soon her face screws up into an angry expression, well, what you can see of her face through the layers of cream paste, the thick blue paint and broad black lines on her eyelids. There is a tiny dark blob on her cheek in the middle of a patch of red which Mum calls rouge. The red on her lips has oozed into the lines under her nose. She stinks of one of those perfumes I play with in Boots when my mother isn't looking. You can spray yourself if they're not in the box. So I did. The assistant hovered and scowled. She knew I didn't have the money. I always look poor with my scuffed Clark's sandals, grubby knees and clothes big enough to last two years.

'You'll grow into it.' I gaze down at the hem in despair. It smells of mothballs and my sister.

Now in Granddad's shop, this lady is huffing and muttering. His usual customers are nice so she can't be one of them.

A few words are exchanged.

'Sorry. Never mind. Special order. Come back another day?'

I keep my head down. I'm in for it. I hear the rustle of her shopping bag, the swish of her full skirt and stiff petticoats, the clickety-click of high heels and, in a final display of rage, the doorbell clangs rather than tinkles.

'Well,' I shrug, 'it isn't my fault. I only tell the truth.'

Granny Weston sweeps the floor with a dustpan and brush but she stretches up holding her back, wipes her brow and frowns. I avoid her glare and look intently at my feet while still kicking the counter. I'm examining the scuffs. It's June, I'm bored with weeks to go until my deaf sister returns from boarding school. I'm sick of playing Patience, squeezing plasticine into rude shapes, bouncing a ball in the garden or talking to Pam my rabbit. That's partly why I said it. You can get away with murder when you're four.

'Granddad looks after his regulars.' Granny's nudging my mum. 'She isn't one of his regulars. She's come 'ere because she can't get it down at Grays.'

'I'll speak to you later.' Mum's face. Oh dear!

In my sister's holidays we play card games such as Snap and Old Maid and board games such as Draughts and Ludo. At Christmas we play Monopoly and Beetle. On fine days, we enjoy our swing, Jokari, (a bat and ball game) where the ball is on elastic fastened to the box, and Jacks. For wet days, there's a special table tennis table which fits over our dining table. Dad made it with painted lines so we can score properly. Well my sister scores. The ping pong ball whizzes past my ear with unfortunate regularity. There's our tepee tent for pretend camping on the back lawn. In the evening, we make believe with the doll's house or Noah's Ark, also made by Dad with wartime wood scraps.

Every day we go out. Each school holiday we visit the deaf twins, Roger and Rosemary, who live near The Ancient Briton – the last but one stop on the 321 route to St Albans. The same bus route takes us to visit Auntie Mac in Rickmansworth. She has two older children, Pauline and Bob. Before her marriage, she was Cissy Hawkins, the daughter and eldest child of my grandmother's elder sister, Sarah.

Some days we take the path opposite Crabtree Lane, to the Common, this being Harpenden's pride and joy, extending the full length of the town from the centre of what we call the Village up to West Common Way, as far as the green belt separating the town from St Albans. The three lower ponds drop down to the right, alongside a path worn down by previous ramblers. A green expanse stretches from the cricket pavilion to where fairs set up on bank holidays. Five minutes later we reach the Silver Cup Pond, out of bounds to my sister and me, as Mum believes it transmits germs. In fact, some blame the polio epidemic on the Silver Cup Pond but I'm unsure it was ever proved, although in the 1970s with Health and Safety policies sweeping the country the pond was filled in, for reasons unclear.

We haven't been in Grove Avenue long. A dark cupboard in the hall holds boxes with numbers. A man comes with book and a torch. To read the gas and electricity meters, Mum says.

My sister and I have had one or two holidays together since we moved. Mum says I'll get holidays when I start school.

I'm feeling happy at the thought.

I didn't like moving, but just as the tummy wobbles began to disappear, everything changes when someone – a neighbour of my grandparents – runs up the path to fetch Mum to my granddad's shop. We have no telephone and neither does my grandmother who goes to the post office if she needs to make a call. I feel a shift in my chest at Mum's frightened face. Mum swoops me up and plonks me in the seat on the back of her bike, pedalling furiously and moaning I'm too big, saying the Lord gave me legs. So next time... She's fit my mum. She did something called The Women's League of Health and Beauty before what they call 'the war'.

He's ill, my granddad, in hospital, can't move on one side. I try it, pretending I can't move on one side to see what it's like, but then someone enters the room.

'What are you doing on the floor?'

'Nothing, only playing.'

I'm not allowed to visit but I keep asking. Whining they call it.

'Please.' It's the fifth time of asking. 'Please can I go to the 'opital?'

Children aren't allowed. Only grown-ups.

I'm not stupid. I know there's trouble with money, nothing much on the shop shelves and men visiting.

'Can I speak to your father?' I hear them murmur to my mother.

One man Mum calls the Chivers rep and another is the Tate and Lyle man who tickles my chin.

'Now who are you?'

I like the Chivers man best – he gives me sweets.

Every night Mum shuts the shop, puts books in her bicycle basket and heads home. They're not library books like mine but exercise books full of figures. There's a bag of money she calls 'takings'. She puts me on her saddle and pushes me home. No, I can't go in the seat.

'You're a dead weight.' It's her way of saying I'm overweight.

'But I am not dead.' I'm serious but she laughs.

Once up our path, Mum runs her finger under the

bottom of the back door and fishes out the door key. Sometimes she lets me get it.

I have to go to bed straightaway. Not just to the bedroom but into my bed with the hard seams down the middle of the bottom sheet. 'Sides to middle' is one of Mum's sewing activities otherwise known as 'make do and mend'. It saves buying new sheets apparently.

My bedroom is hot and stuffy and I can't sleep so I peep out of the window. Darkness hasn't yet arrived and children from the council houses stand outside popping their heads above the hedge, dodging down if I look out.

'Hey you!' they shout, calling my name. I wonder how they know. I haven't started school yet.

Mum and Dad hear them and call upstairs telling me to get back to bed AT ONCE. They have the radio on for *Ray's A Laugh* so 'don't want no nonsense'. They're laughing but I'm not allowed to join in.

'Some bits are rude,' says Mum.

Often, I see what they are up to before I go upstairs. They're counting the halfpennies, pennies and thrupenny bits, separating sixpences, shillings, florins and half crowns. They even count the farthings! They lick fingers and flick through the ten bob and pound notes. Mum writes doodles in her book and, when I'm in bed, I hear her slam it down.

'Bloody hell!' What? She tells me off if I use bad language.

Sometimes, if I can't sleep, I sit on the top stair and listen. I hear Mum saying it's difficult to get things. Something called supplies.

Then my dad's voice, soothing, kind, as always.

'Don't worry. Just pay off some money so you can buy a few things for the shelves, take names and orders from people and it'll all be fine. I'll help you.'

Yes, he would.

I hear Mum saying, 'No, what are we going to do about my dad when he comes out of hospital? He won't get better. Whatever will we do with Mum then?'

I don't want to hear any more. Scary thoughts flutter by my head. I stagger back to bed and creep under the covers. Tears dribble down my cheeks and soak into my pillow. I hadn't realised Granddad was so ill. I miss his twinkly smile, little jokes and loving pats on the head. He fusses me more than Mum or Dad.

Sometimes I think, secretly, that if my granddad has a favourite... well I know it's naughty to think like that, but if he does, then, I think it's probably me.

One day I'm behind the shop counter with my dolly. There are shelves where large jars are waiting for sweets to go off ration. Granddad said, 'When all this silly business is over,' I will learn to weigh them like I weigh broken biscuits. I want him to come back home. I keep asking when but the adults just say, 'Stop asking.'

The doorbell tinkles and it's one of my uncles. Granny's sniffing and her face is blotchy. He gives her money. She pushes it away shaking her head, saying, 'No you can't do that,' but he says, 'You're my sister after all. That's what families are for. I have to help you.' Granny wraps her arms round him. She needs to go on tiptoe. Then she makes me a fish paste sandwich. She knows what I like.

At dinner, Dad says, 'The shop will have to be put up for sale at some stage but you'll get a better price if it's doing well.'

Another day I look up to find the sugar man peering over the counter.

'Hello, Dinah. How are you today?'

I don't answer. Mum told me not to talk to strange men.

Granddad owes him money. He leans across the counter to my mother. He says it quietly but I hear everything. Apparently I have big ears. The Tate and Lyle man promises more treacle and sugar as well as goodies for the posh customers.

Oh I love treacle.

Customers ask Mum about Granddad.

'How much longer?'

She says my grandmother can't cope.

'But she can,' I want to shout. 'She keeps sweeping with her dustpan and brush.'

You see, I really want to be at home playing in my den.

'She needs me here.' My heart sinks.

One lady has moved from London. She tells Mum there's more choice in the shops there. When she leaves, Mum says, 'She'd better go back there then.' She was fat with wobbly bits on her tummy and her bust drooping down to her waist.

No-one in our family is fat. We don't have much on our plate at dinner and no-one ever says anything is bad for us. That is except the dentist, Mr Smiley Face, who I hate. He says sugar is bad for our teeth. I don't care. We eat white bread, sprinkle white sugar on our cereals. Flour is white, the only difference being plain or self-raising. Food is still what they call 'scarce' and many foods are rationed until 1954. Bread and jam aren't on ration now but tea is still rationed and, although I don't know then, it will be until 1952. Not that I am interested in bread and tea. All we children think about is sweets.

Just in time for my fourth birthday, sweets go off ration. For a while we have as much as we're allowed which, in our house, isn't much. Everyone's talking about it, getting excited and running down to Southdown sweetshop. Joy is in the air with pear drops, jelly babies and aniseed balls. Also toffees, liquorice and more! Then almost as suddenly, they disappear.

'Everyone's gone mad,' Granddad says.

Secretly I think I'd like the opportunity to go mad if it means eating sweets but my mother stays tight-lipped and I sense some relief in her manner when they're restricted again. She doesn't want more arguments with Mr Smiley Face.

My Uncle Frank rushes into the shop one day, shaking his head. He's between jobs whatever that means.

'The small shop is dead,' he shouts. 'Sainsbury's has opened.

Not in Harpenden, I think. I would've known.

'It's only a matter of time,' he says, 'before supermarkets come. They've got them in London. People serve themselves.'

How can people do that? I wonder. Surely they can't go round the back of the counter where I have my dollies and teddies, just take things and put money in the little wooden till. What if they didn't put enough in?

Perhaps it will be like Woolworth's in the Village where Mum takes me for penny sweets. You pick up what you want and hand it to the girl.

One day a customer with a dark face comes in. She speaks in a funny voice and asks my mother for food with strange names. Mum calls her coloured. We see people like that when we go to London but I've never seen one in Harpenden.

I love travelling in London on the Underground. The railway porters, ticket collectors and cleaners are black skinned. I don't understand a word they say. But I'd love curly hair like that. Mum says they come from Jamaica like the bananas.

'Your sister didn't see a banana until she was seven years old.'

Mum doesn't speak to what Granny calls 'darkies' unless she has to. Luckily, she knows her way around but, if she's stuck, or if there are engineering works or a platform is closed, she asks for help.

My cousin does train-spotting, collecting the names and numbers of the trains. British Railways' trains never run on time. We're always hanging about on the platform waiting for the man with the red flag to wave it at the driver. We hear it coming, its whistle and a loud *CHOOO* as it comes in from St Pancras. The driver hangs out of his door, whistles to Mum and calls out.

'Give us a kiss, darling!'

Her face goes red.

I can't take my eyes off the large black woman Mum calls a foreigner who works in the station's smelly toilets. Back in Granddad's shop some dark people have started coming in. Granddad is nice to them but Granny pulls a face. I know she doesn't like them. They want food we don't grow in England.

'Stuff that makes their breath pong,' says Granny.

Not Bird's blancmange or jelly then?

'It's all changed since the war.' Mum and Granny talk all the time about how things used to be and why everything is different. Italians and some Germans from the prisoner of war camp at Batford wander around. They are all free now and want special food.

Granny says, 'It's all those people who ran from 'itler. That's the trouble.'

I see Mum scowl, her shoulders stiffen and she mutters something to Granny about speaking properly in front of me and sounding her aiches. She thinks they're common – the folks who don't say the haich.

Somehow I don't think 'itler is a rep.

I don't enjoy the shop so much now. Before Granddad was ill, he let me get bits and bobs, as he calls them, from the shelf, put things in brown paper bags and give change to customers. He gave me broken biscuits to weigh, which he sold cheap. Some days he takes me to the post office to put 'a bob on the horses' but he tells Granny he's going for change for the till.

Granddad has a bike with a big metal basket on and a boy comes on a Wednesday to do deliveries of cardboard packets, lemonade, Tizer and a few tins plus bags of biscuits and eggs. The boy returns with empty bottles and Granddad takes some money off their next bill. If the boy is ill, Granddad takes the bike himself.

'I am off to see my lovely ladies,' he chirps as he skips out the door.

But, now he's in hospital and his lovely ladies miss him. They used to ask for things and sometimes he could find it hidden somewhere.

'Don't tell.' He winks at them.

'Lots of shortages and there's still rationing,' he says to the ones he doesn't like.

'What's rationing?' I ask.

Apparently, we can only have so much food each because in the war the German submarines sank the food boats.

'But it's not the war now.'

'No, but the factories are busy making other more important things.'

'Such as?'

Granddad says there are electrical items which work from a plug in the wall. The posh lady from further down Southdown Road likes electrical things. She has a heater for the bathroom and something she holds in her hand that blows hot air on her hair. That would be better than sitting with my back to the fire, I reckon.

'Can we have them? My sweets are on ration,' I say. I can only have a few and I have to show my book.

'That's right.' Granddad likes kids who ask questions. Well, some food still needs tickets. I know that.

All the lady customers think Granddad's handsome. His hair is red like Mum's and his nose is freckly. He has his favourite customers and tells jokes. Mum says he's a flirt and ought to act his age. I don't know how old he is but I remember a party when he was sixty.

In the shop, sometimes, he hides items under the counter.

'They're for my lady friend,' he whispers, when he sees me looking. Then he winks at me with his twinkly eyes. That was where I saw the sugar the lady wanted.

One lady shows Mum her new cookery book – Elizabeth David.

'I'll try ordering,' Mum promises. 'What is it?' I ask. Mum says, 'Pasta.' We don't eat that.

The next day another rep with hair on his lip says he'll try to bring what she needs for her posh customers. That's what Mum calls people with money.

They're all cooking French stuff and fancy meals.

'Like what?' I ask.

'Snails!' Mum is laughing but my stomach heaves. Surely people don't eat them.

'We can't get everything they want.' The rep is twiddling his moustache.

I can't take my eyes off it.

A Narrow Escape

My dad always cycled home for lunch soon after one o'clock and I was in the habit of saying to my mother that I was going down the road to 'wait for Daddy' and then wandering down to the bottom of the road. Further along from Grove Avenue there was a wooden bench seat at the foot of a winding lane which weaved its way behind the houses on the opposite side of our road. People who lived on the opposite side of Grove Avenue had the benefit of a gate or other access to this lane which was used for dog-walking or for teenagers to play Cowboys and Indians.

I must have been a regular lunchtime sight. Harpenden and, more so, South Harpenden, was a small village in those days and few women worked outside the home. It's amazing to think that I was allowed out alone but I was usually kept back until my father was expected to be within easy reach of the house. Immediately he came along I would be lifted up and placed on the crossbar and wheeled up the road to home.

One day my father was later than usual and, instead of his familiar face arriving on his bicycle, a boy much older than myself came cycling by and, after passing me, he turned his wheels full circle, riding back to pull up sharply alongside where I was sitting on the bench. He began to speak to me but I'd been told not to talk to strangers and at first I was reticent but, after asking me what I was doing and receiving the answer that I was 'waiting for my daddy', he said that he had a message from my father that I had to go with him and he would meet up with both of us later. I began to protest but he was very persuasive and insistent telling me that my father would be very cross if I did not do as he said.

'I know your daddy very well,' he says, 'and he says it is very important that you do as I say.'

I still hesitate.

'Your daddy said he would be cross if you don't do as I say,' he said. Not wishing to be the object of my father's disapproval I began to follow him, albeit reluctantly, slowly up the lane – he pushing his bike and repeating the message that I would be in trouble if I didn't do as he said. His charming, yet firm voice was convincing and all I was aware of was the sight of his Fair Isle jumper combined with the flickering sun through the trees and bushes which evoked a strange feeling, almost surreal.

It never occurred to me to turn on my heels and run back down the lane, although fear was beginning to ripple through my body and my heart was pounding like a drum although I didn't know why. Suddenly, my independent air and confidence had fled leaving me timid and weak. After some time, I realised we had gone a long way and a quick glance back showed the road now frighteningly out of view.

Along the path there were grassy banks and clearings and he stopped at one of these and pushed me forward to go into one with him. Just at that moment, there was the sound of crackling undergrowth, movement behind the trees, then barking followed by a shout.

'What's going on here?'

At great speed the boy grabbed his bicycle and ran off jumping on to his bicycle when he was halfway down the lane and with the dog barking and snarling at his heels.

This man, I am sure, saved my life. Bob was the husband of my mother's close friend, Nan, who lived further up Grove Avenue. He was home for lunch and always took his Alsatian for a walk.

When the boy was out of view, he returned to where I was standing shaking.

'Are you all right?' he asked.

I nodded and he beckoned me to come with him and the dog to his rear garden gate. Once in his garden he let the dog run loose and we walked past his vegetable garden towards the back of his house.

Nan, his wife, was a comforting sight.

'You must go down and tell them what you saw!' she said when he told her what he had found. So that's what happened next. Bob took me home.

'Look what I've found and guess where she was?' he said. My father was eating his dinner and my mum was busy in the kitchen.

Initially, they looked cross that I had not waited for Dad where I usually did but Bob told them what he saw and how he chased the young lad down the lane.

'The dog nearly got him,' he said. I watched their faces change to horror. In those days it was unheard of for children to be in danger so near to home. Somewhat traumatised, I expected their disapproval, but soon realised they were upset. It could have easily ended up differently. I sat and ate my dinner in silence after which the police arrived and I was questioned by a policewoman.

In 1950 child abduction was unusual although a *Good Housekeeping* magazine in 1953, did report a rise in offences against girls under sixteen in the years immediately following 1945. It is possible such incidents always happened but weren't talked about. At home this became the 'elephant in the room' and was never spoken of again but I was well aware I'd had a lucky escape.

September 1950

'I don't think I'll go today.'

Wednesday, my third day at school and my mother finds me still in bed.

'But you have to go every day.'

'Whaaat? Do you mean every day, every time I wake up?'

'Yes, get up and get into your school clothes.'

Oh no, I think, not again … not those awful clothes. No-one else wears school uniform. Our headmistress, says there isn't a proper school uniform but we can, if our mothers want to buy them, wear white blouses and navy skirts. Well, Mum doesn't just get me a skirt; she gets me something she calls a pinafore – similar to what the lady wears in the chemist.

Mum never misses anything.

'What's that look for?'

If my face looks bad before I leave home, it's ten times worse at the end of my first day when I realise no-one else wears navy. Their mothers didn't ask about uniform.

On the second day, a few of the other girls give me funny looks. They wear pretty knitted cardigans with lots of holes that are meant to be there. Any holes in my navy cardigan are there by accident and, when I find one, I need a very good excuse for Mum. One day I play chase in the playground when a boy catches my cardigan sleeve gripping it tight. To my horror, the sleeve begins to get a large hole until it falls away from my arm and droops down almost to the ground.

Oh heck, what am I to do?

My legs wobble like jelly and shake as I approach my mother at the school gate. She's standing with other parents.

To my surprise the expected telling off doesn't happen. I can't believe what I'm hearing.

'Never mind, it's old anyway and you need a new one,' she says.

The knot in my tummy goes away and relief floods my body like a warm bath. The breath I am holding begins to escape. A smile creeps across my face and I stop gripping the straps of my satchel.

Oh that satchel! That's another thing that makes me different. No-one else has a satchel and, if they have a bag it isn't a real leather one. When I say mine is real leather, this is a hot topic in class.

'You mean it's made from a COW?' Mary is what I think they call gobsmacked.

'Golly gosh,' she says.

'Will it moo?' They're sniggering.

'What's it for?' They're coming up and touching it and squeezing it.

When I answer, their laughter fills the air. No-one wants a bag for BOOKS.

But, what I want more than anything is a friend. My chest heaves. It's sad without anyone to giggle with. At home, my friends in the road come to knock on my back door and ask to play. But, they haven't started school yet.

Douglas is a neighbour and keen to be a friend. That is until the day he helps himself to a spade in the shed, digs up my father's precious apple tree from the side of the house and replants it in the middle of our new lawn.

My mother spots him through the kitchen window.

'What are you doing Douglas?'

'Giving you some shade on your lawn, Mrs Munt.'

My mother places the blame for the large hole in the lawn and a wilting branch that was the new apple tree firmly in my lap.

'Daddy's plants are special.'

Where my tattered cardigan is concerned, I just hope Mum hasn't said it doesn't matter just for show. Sometimes she pretends to be nice and saves up the telling off when we come through the door.

We use our back door. The front door is only for visitors and gypsies who sell bunches of heather.

'Sixpence to cross your palm and have your fortune told?'

'No.' Mum's face speaks volumes.

'Fortune, what's that?'

I've never heard of it before.

Granny doesn't do that either.

The fortune thing.

'Just live for today,' she sniffs. 'The H-bomb will get us soon.'

Not only do the other girls have pretty knitted things, they have shop-bought bright white socks which don't have holes sewn up with wool – something Mum calls darning. Also they have pretty ribbons in their hair.

'Can't I have a ribbon?' I ask my mum after my first day.

'Why? You don't need one, your hair's short.'

That heart-sink feeling again. I feel sick in my throat. My mother is always having my hair cut. Just when it looks nice and I flick it behind my ear or twiddle it into a curl, she carts me off to the hairdresser near Mr Conrath's butcher shop.

'Just started school,' says Mum to the young blonde girl who beckons me to a chair.

'Do you want much off?' asks Blondie.

'No.' Me.

'Yes.' Mum.

'Why do I have to have so much cut off?' I ask, my voice turning to sobs, a solitary tear streaking down my cheek.

'I don't want to have to bring you back in a few weeks,' Mum lowers her voice, 'not at these prices.'

In the mirror I see the girl – her name is Wendy – look at me with a sympathetic smile and I don't feel so bad after that.

'Is that enough?' Wendy's stopped snipping.

'Yes.'

'No,' Mum says. 'Take more off her fringe.'

'Not my fringe,' I wail. 'Please, please!'

But chop, chop, until my head resembles a scrubbing brush. I want to cry and I do, later in my room, after I am sent to bed for being cheeky and arguing with Mum in front of Wendy.

* * *

I don't have to go to the shop every day now. It isn't summer anymore. I have to learn my letters and start writing to my sister. Mum, always late, lifts me into the seat on the back of her bike and cycles furiously along Southdown Road. It's quicker that way.

Because, she says, you dawdle. She leaves me at the school gate and hurries across the road to Granddad's shop to start serving customers.

At half past three, Mum is waiting at the gate ready to take me back to the shop. Here I find dolly and teddy behind the counter are pleased to see me.

Every Saturday Mum takes me to the shop and customers ask me the same question.
'Hello, Dinah. How do you like school?'
'Isall right.'
'Speak clearly, Dinah,' says Mum.

Soon after Bonfire Night, we don't have to go to the shop any more.
It's sold.
The new owners have a son, David, who starts in my class at St John's. Mr Spacey's van comes to take all my

grandparents' furniture and move it to a flat above Dad's shop in the Village.

Now Mum brings me straight home from school and runs her finger under the back door where the key sits. I like to run up the hill, charge through the gate and fumble for the hidden key before Mum gets near. When my sister's home we race each other. There's a side gate so no-one sees us hide the key. It stays there all day.

'Shut the gate so the spivs don't see where we hide the key,' Mum says. I am not to speak to them, she adds.
The spivs wear trilby hats and tight trousers. Their cigarettes turn down to face the pavement as ash seeps upwards and into their mouths.

But life in South Harpenden is good. We can go up Walkers Road and in minutes we are in awe of the Common and its delights. Our favourite is an outing to the Prickle Dells, named after the abundant large gorse bushes. We leave the path near St John's Road, and once in the Dells, run up and down the winding, narrow, little paths, getting lost before finding our way out again – our very own Hampton Court Maze. Within minutes our lives are transformed into a fantasy world of Cowboys and Indians, the Lone Ranger and Hopalong Cassidy. Some children call these the 'ups and downs'.

By now, Granddad is home from hospital but he isn't as jolly. He sits in a chair all the time and often falls asleep. I sit and talk to him but Mum frowns.

'Dinah, leave Granddad alone.'
'Why?'
'He's tired. Stop talking such rubbish.'
'But Granddad likes my stories.'

Starting School

St John's infants' school sits proudly on Southdown Road, directly opposite the Triangle – a grassy area where big boys and girls are allowed to play in the evening. Its tarmac playground spreads itself to the footpath, a simple fence keeping us in. The headmistress, Miss Swann, travels to Southdown by the 321 bus with her cocker spaniel, Andy, who snoozes in a basket under her desk.

I am five years old and it's the first time I've been away from my mother. She's always at home.

'There are no jobs,' she moans. 'They've all gone to the men who came back from the war.'

'I did work,' she adds, 'at de Havilland aircraft factory, ordering spare parts for the Mosquito fighters.'

Our first teacher, Miss W, has a serious face. We sit in the same classroom all day, every day, a packed room with fifty children. We are the Bulge – the post-war babies. To squeeze everyone in we sit in rows facing the board chanting out letters and sounds and our first times tables. There's little chance for fun except when we are let out in the playground. At morning playtime we drink a small bottle of milk with a straw. The teachers stand over us until it has all gone.

'It's good for your teeth.'

One boy tells our teacher the date every morning. When she asks I don't raise my hand. I don't even know it's November. I had my birthday in September. I wasn't asked what I wanted. I had to take what I got according to my mother ... and remember to say thank you. At school, on my birthday I kept quiet. I didn't want the bumps.

I think Miss W is really old until my dad calls her 'a pretty little thing', following their first parents' evening. Mum snorts in disgust but he just laughs.

One day, Miss W asks this same boy how he knows the date.

'It's on the front page of the newspaper, Miss.' His family have a newspaper delivered every day. It has a name I haven't heard before.

'Whereabouts?' Miss W asks.

That'll fool him, I think.

'Top right hand corner. Just under the name of the paper, Miss.'

Wow, what a mouthful. Strange I don't know this. *The Daily Express* drops through our letter box at breakfast time but I've yet to be shown the date. Surprising that, as Mum has high hopes educationally for both my sister and me.

If I ask what's in the paper, my parents say, 'Lots of trouble in the world, nothing worth reading, better to read a book,' which I think is a bit odd as they sit every evening reading the *Evening News* page by page. They even divide the sheets between them. The only part of the *Express* I read is the cartoon on the back page below the sport.

'Does anyone else read any part of a newspaper?'

I reckon I could answer that. I hate being the odd one out. I want to die because of the awful pinafore. I think I might get some of the girls to play with me if I sound like I have a normal home after all. So I have a go.

My hand shoots up and Miss W looks across the desks peering over her spectacles with a surprised expression because the funny girl who's the only one in uniform is going to speak at last.

'I do, Miss,' I say eagerly.

'What do you read, Dinah?'

'The Gambols, Miss.'

Really? Hmmm. Miss W is staring at my scrubbing-brush haircut.

A deathly silence hangs over the room. I am not sure if what I said might warrant a ticking off or even a smack. The swotty boy clearly has never been introduced to the Gambols and no-one else seems interested. What a waste of effort! I wish I hadn't bothered.

'We 'as comics, Miss,' says one of the boys.

'A comic, my boy,' says Miss Ward, 'is not going to get you very far in life.'

That's right, I think. Comics are not allowed at home.

'My dad does the pools, Miss,' says David. 'And 'e checks 'm in the paper on a Sunday morning.'

Miss W looks across the room at David.

'Well, David, I don't think we need to talk about the Football Pools at the moment.'

'Why not, Miss?' David says. 'Old Mrs Flannagan's husband won fifty quid the other week.'

'Do you know, my boy, what the Pools are?'

David shakes his head.

'It's gambling, David.' Then taking a deep breath so that she can talk without gasping, she adds, 'And that's a terrible waste of money.'

I am about to say that my dad does Littlewoods Pools every Saturday and he says we'll go on holiday on the train to Clacton if we win, but I think better of it now. Every Saturday evening he sits by the radio cabinet, switches it on and marks his coupon with the scores. He's not a frightening man, but it's more than my life's worth to make any noise. I know the treble chance is the best. Dad says you'd get about £7,800 if you win that.

When the Pools man on the radio has finished, Dad waits for the *Light Programme*. My parents take the *Radio Times*. Mum doesn't want to listen to *Twenty Questions* with Gilbert Harding.

All this Pools business must remain a secret or I will get that look from Miss W – a look of another soul lost to God's path or worse, like the look she gave me when I said the Gambols. It shows what she thinks of me. I see her make notes alongside our names.

I must be on her devil list.

I shall never get to heaven.

September 1951 – Statty Fair

'Can we go to the fair?'

We are so excited when the first caravan or lorry appears on the Common a few days before a bank holiday.

'Save up your coppers,' Mum reminds me.

Dad always has some pennies and thrupenny bits in his pocket. He takes us on the dodgem cars. Toffee apples and candyfloss await. My mouth waters already.

We go to the Common near the Silver Cup Pond, before the Baa Lamb trees, named, according to Mum, because in the 1800s sheep grazed beneath those trees in the shade under the watchful eye of their shepherd. The 238 acre common is known as Harpenden's pride and joy.

But, as well as bank holiday fairs we have a regular one on the second Tuesday and Wednesday of September known as the Statty Fair, so called as it's a Statute Fair, i.e. provided by law. This is always the biggest fair and the one most eagerly anticipated.

The noise and bustle rings in my ears. Familiar tunes play loudly and the clang of bells sounds when a ride stops and starts. Every van and caravan hums with electricity. When Dad was small, the lights were from gas but now there are steam-driven generators that make electric. The steam engines draw their water from the ponds. Children and young adults enjoy the roundabouts, the cake walk, the swings and coconut shies. There are sideshows with swarthy men to take your money.

I'm not sure about the swing boats, the dodgem cars and other fun rides. I don't like those that go high.

'You can go on the hoopla,' Mum nods.

'Not the firing ranges?' Mum shakes her head.

I ride home on my dad's shoulders clutching his thick wavy hair so I don't fall.

October 1951 – Harvest Festival

Mum calls the garden my father's other woman. 'It's the only love affair he's had since marrying me,' she says.

The pinafore, ragged cardigan and lace up Start-Rite shoes make me a laughing stock at school but there's worse.
'Flowers. Yes.' Dad's smiling. 'We have loads.' Everywhere we go on our outings, special places such as Bernard Shaw's house, my father twists off new shoots on plant stems or pulls a sprouting from the ground. He looks round furtively, tells me to stand behind him to block the caretaker's view, stuffs the green things or brown twiggy bits in his pocket. Once home he empties his pockets and disappears. The cloches down the garden keep plants warm while they grow. A brick garden frame has an old window which lifts up for watering.

His garden fills with plants. Every week packets of seeds arrive through the post. Dad sets rows, thins them and asks me to water them. The front garden has stocks, hollyhocks, montbretia and others. Dad teaches me the names of the plants.

Now it's Monday morning, so I am given flowers from Dad's garden to take to school. Not just a few little ones but an enormous bunch nearly as tall as I am. I have 3/6d dinner money in my satchel but nothing else.

'He loves his garden,' Mum says. 'The bunch is a bouquet,' she adds.

I cringe when carrying these flowers and school mates eye me up and down. My cheeks feel hot when I see kids I know. I can't see the ground through the stalks. Sometimes a car passes slowly and those inside stare and point.

My legs drag like two bags of Tate and Lyle sugar as I trudge through the playground and my tummy feels fluttery when the day's monitor rings the hand bell. I bump into other children. My mouth dries up. If someone asks where the flowers come from I only squeak.

But, hurray, there's an upside to this horrid start to the week. Each Monday I am allowed to fetch a large jug from the other classroom cupboard, fill it with water and arrange the flowers. I take my time.

I return with the jug of water holding the flowers and place the vase in full view of the class, usually on the teacher's table. My classmates have their heads down doing the sums the teacher has written on the board.

This is when it's worth it.

You see, if I am slow – really slow – I can make this job last for at least twenty minutes. Then on sitting down, I pretend not to know what I should be doing which can account for a further ten minutes flicking the pages of my exercise book and gazing in bewilderment at the blackboard.

Stop! Miss W calls for all pencils to be put down.

Not finished? I did the flowers, Miss. Right.

The cupboard with the jugs is the same one where the teachers keep the toilet roll. They give it out three pieces at a time, which is definitely not enough for my wobbly tummy. The paper is hard and scratchy. One day I go in during playtime feeling my poo might start any minute. I rush in, open the cupboard, pull a long trail and head off outside.

'Stop! You've enough for a whole class there!'

I need it, I think. I've crossed my legs.

It's urgent I try to say but the teacher doesn't hear or doesn't want to. She lets me go with a few pieces by which time it's too late.

If I can, I put off going to the lavatory at school. They smell of wee and the concrete floors are wet. I can hardly reach the chain which dangles from a box near the ceiling.

The toilets don't all have doors; some have a half door hanging off the hinge. In winter the pan has solid ice but when you wee it melts it on the top and leaves a yellow stain. On frosty mornings the chain won't flush either. Your Number Two sits curled and smiles up at you when you finish.

At the end of playtime a teacher shakes the bell and we line up outside the door. Once inside, Miss W writes in chalk on the board and sometimes the white stick breaks when she's in the middle of something. If you snigger softly you might get away with it. Otherwise, teachers use chalk as missiles and send them flying towards the naughty boys.

Not content with a bunch of flowers that make me an object of scorn, my father also teaches me the names of the plants, so that, if asked, I can name them. But no sooner am I on Grove Road than I forget. Even the common names escape me. If I do remember I only do it once. The bigger boys at the back of the class mutter 'teacher's pet' and then chant it all through playtime. It's best to look as if you can't hear. You get more friends that way.

In October, we plod in a line up Walkers Road, under the railway bridge for the Harvest Festival at St John's church in St John's Road. At the service, every child brings food made or grown at home for Harvest Festival. My father digs up some vegetables, pulls a lettuce and cuts more flowers. I stumble, arms full, down Grove Avenue, into Grove Road.

Before the service, we assemble in the school playground. Oh nice, an extra few minutes of play. But then the bell rings out ending all our fun. We carry all our items up Walkers Road and turn left into St John's Road. Just opposite the Prickle Dells is St John's Church. The Dells is where Mum takes us in the holidays so we can run around and do something called 'get it all out your system'.

Once in church we file into the front rows of the nave, sit on hard wooden seats and listen to the vicar telling us the meaning of Harvest Festival. Some parents are there. Mum finds her best clothes and earrings which she only wears on special occasions.

On the floor in front of our wooden seats a blue cushion called a hassock is for kneeling down to say prayers. We stand to sing hymns. We bellow 'We Plough the Fields and Scatter' but some boys sing a rude version. During one hymn we take our produce to the chancel steps. The vicar tells us our gifts will be taken to old people's homes and to the homes of the poor. Strange that. I thought we were poor but Mum shakes her head.

'You don't know the half of it. We think we're poor but there are people who have no shoes for their feet.'

Well, I've never seen anyone like that. I know a little bit about poor people. Granddad Weston's family didn't have enough shoes to go round twelve children.

'First up, best dressed,' he says, 'and you never took a jumper off in the house or you wouldn't see it again. The only ones who went to school were those who found a pair of shoes to fit.' Oh I love Granddad's stories of life before I was born.

Granddad and his brothers – there were eleven brothers and one sister in the Weston family – were brought up on a farm at the top of Piggotshill Lane. Not much to do, he says, other than mope about the farm or go down to the Village and get into trouble. Not bad trouble with the local bobby but mischief such as sending the copper on a wild goose chase or playing *Knock Down Jenny* in a row of terraced cottages. The art was to tie string to all the door knockers and then disappear round the corner. One tug on the string caused the knockers to bang on the doors and all the housewives bedecked in large aprons would poke their noses out of the door, look cross, shout at the kids running away round the corner, then disappear inside slamming the door so hard the windows shook.

The Harvest Festival doesn't last long. It reminds me how much I'd have loved to grow up on a farm. My dream was to live on a smallholding with animals grunting and mooing plus growing vegetables. Life now in 1951 is so different to Granddad's. To me, being poor is not having fluffy lacy cardigans. Somehow, if your father grows vegetables and has fruit trees in the garden, you are considered well off. When I come home from the Harvest Festival, I make sure I tell Dad his produce was well received. He'd be hurt if I didn't.

On the way out of church I see Mum talking to some of the St John's Young Wives. The club was started by the vicar's wife and we have a summer tea party in the vicarage garden. Mum has put on her posh voice and is talking about my sister.

Mrs Potts says, 'Oh dear, oh dear.'

Someone has suggested a cinema outing at half term. Mum shakes her head. Cinema isn't good visual entertainment for my deaf sister.

The year after I start school everyone's talking about the Festival of Britain. We learn about it at school. Dad says it's to celebrate everything Britain has made since the war. We learn about the war and how hard life was after it ended. Our teacher tells us the Festival is to mark the anniversary of the First Great Exhibition in 1851. We have some time off school to enjoy the fun. The week-long celebrations are mentioned in *The Times* so Dad buys that paper rather than the *Express*. There are races in the High Street; a ladies' pram race and a men's barrel-rolling event. Everyone is laughing and shouting to their children to get on with it!

We go to the Festival fair on the Common, a boys' soap box derby and a girls' hoop race. The Festival takes place in the summer and one night, after the fireworks, I come back across the Common sitting on Dad's shoulders. I've never been happier, especially as a trip to London by train is being planned. The Tuffins, Westons and Hawkins love going to London for special events; Coronations, royal occasions, weddings, Trooping the Colour and other parades. The steam train whizzes us to St Pancras and we cross the city by Tube to a park where there are roundabouts and large wheels.

November

Firework Night is a special occasion. Excitement buzzes. The shops fill with roman candles, bangers, sparklers, rockets and others and my sister's home on half term. When Dad

is ready to do the display, we're sent to Mum and Dad's bedroom where we watch with our noses pressed so hard against the glass they leave imprints on the glass in the circle of steam from hot excited breath.

Sometimes a firework doesn't go off straightaway but Dad is careful not to return to a failed smouldering lump of gunpowder. He uses a long garden cane to knock it out of the way; on hand, a pail of sand and a bucket of water for emergencies. When he is sure a failed firework is safe, he attempts to re-light it. Catherine wheels are nailed to the side of an orange box, so named as they stored imported oranges. In post-war Britain, with wood in short supply, some people painted them as bedside tables. I always had one or two in my den.

I am beginning to enjoy school. A few children now have blouses and ties like mine. Mum told their mothers where mine came from. So it's not all bad. Some lessons are sheer joy. I love music, singing, banging cymbals and flicking castanets. Even better is the afternoon story. But writing is my favourite. From the moment I hold a pencil, I am fascinated with the written word and the fairy tale world I can produce straight out of my head. It's so much better than life as I know it.

'She writes good stories,' my teacher tells my mother at parents' evening but my mother is unimpressed. She's only interested in whether I can do arithmetic and spell. She hasn't forgotten My Life Story.

But now I begin writing stories at school too. They are lengthy – I can't stop – and they serve to save me from miserable outside play on a cold winter day. I like to show my teacher how enthusiastic I am about English. She thinks she has a literary genius in her class at last. Having asked to stay in to finish my story, the answer is always yes and I keep scribbling (what Mum calls it). Desperate to avoid the frosty or waterlogged outside space, I keep my head down with pencil poised over the page and wait until my red-nosed, blue- lipped class mates return frozen-toed from the icy wastes of the infant playground before I write with a flourish …

The End.

Coronation 1953

Yesterday we were all sent home early from school because the King had died. Today, I come downstairs and hear sniffing. My parents sit with stiff backs, their faces sad.

Dad says, 'We will have a coronation soon.' When a King or Queen dies, he explains, their eldest son would be crowned King but if they only had a daughter, she would be crowned Queen. Apparently King George became King because his older brother, Edward, wanted to marry a divorcee, but he couldn't so he abdicated.

At school everyone is talking about the King's death. Our teacher tells us that Elizabeth will be Queen now.

It's February and cold. Princess Elizabeth has returned from a foreign tour and steps off the plane dressed in black. The funeral is reported on the radio and, soon after, we go to the cinema and see film of it on Pathé News. Crowds line the streets as a gun carriage carries him to Westminster Abbey. Sobs can be heard all over the Mall.

Mum says that, in the war, the King and Queen visited the people in the East End of London who had been bombed.

'Yes.' Granny nods. 'They had the chance to leave London but they chose to stay and support the people.'

After King George's death, his wife, Queen Elizabeth, becomes known as the Queen Mother. She's Granny's favourite Royal. On special days, my family take the train to London and walk down the Mall to Buckingham Palace in the hope of seeing the King and Queen on the balcony. Any special event and we're off to London and we've photographs to prove it.

* * *

After Granddad's stroke, my grandparents can't manage the shop and life on two floors above the grocer's is impractical. Mum manages the shop until it's sold and my grandparents move to a flat above my father's shop in Station Road. We call the main part of Harpenden 'The Village'.

In the back room behind the shop a door leads to the flat via a stairway to a lower landing and, beyond that, stairs lead to a bedroom and a living room. At the top, before the lounge, is the kitchen which only has a gas cooker and a sink. A screen hides the toilet. They have no bathroom; hot water is from a geezer over a sink, which is also used as a wash basin.

'How do you have a bath?' I ask.

'We don't have baths.' A smile flickers as Granny watches my reaction. 'Granddad and I have a strip wash every other day.' I don't ask more questions.

Every morning, Dad goes to the newsagent on the corner of Station Road for his twenty Senior Service cigarettes. Sometimes he pops into the estate agents – Brading and Harmer. He and Phil Harmer were at school together.

At number 5 is a butcher's shop where Saturday boys are employed. My grandmother's garden, at the rear of the parade of shops, is a picture of flowers. A passageway leads along the back of the shops and at the far end we turn left down a passageway by the post office. There are steps up to the post office. The next shop is Harpenden Dairies. The front windows of Granny's flat overlook Station Road and the High Street. She sits and watches people pass by, many of whom she knows from her childhood days.

* * *

In the school holidays my sister, Susan, and I are sent out to the Southdown shops with a list including a loaf of bread – a large home-made – from Ackroyd's bakers, about four or five shops to the left of Spackman's Chemist. After this chemist there's the post office.

In the butcher's Susan and I ask for the meat. We get it from Mr Conrath and then pay Mrs Conrath at the kiosk. This system ensures good hygiene as the butcher doesn't handle money. Next to the wool shop there's a hardware store, Marsh and Russell. Sometimes Dad sends one of us there to buy a sheet of sandpaper. In Deal's wool shop we ask for a couple of ounces of Mum's wool that's been set aside to spread the cost. Sometimes we have to ask for a packet of Dr White's size 2, without understanding what they are. Mrs Deal puts them in a brown paper bag so no-one can see what we've bought.

Opposite Ackroyd's baker shop there is the Methodist church. To the right, Gibbons shoe shop and Fullilove's sweet and paper shop. Another grocer shop, Grays, stands between Westons and the butcher. Lastly, and, because we're lugging heavy purchases, we visit Reads greengrocer, on the corner of Cravells Road.

Granddad's Stories

I look at Granddad. 'What did you do in the war?'

He tells me he didn't fight in the Second World War as he was too old. He was an ARP (Air Raid Precautions) warden. An ARP Warden's main task was to try and protect people during air raids, when enemy planes dropped bombs, especially on cities. He would shout *PUT THAT LIGHT OUT* during the blackout when people had to cover their windows.

In the First World War he was in The Essex Regiment. He shows me a photograph of himself wearing army uniform and what he calls a trench coat. He looks cold but he's smiling. The photo was put on a postcard and sent to my granny.

He took part in raiding parties, when soldiers crept out of their trenches and slipped into those of the Germans.

'They never asked for volunteers. They'd say you, you, you and you, and then you suddenly found yourself in a raiding party.' They crawled underneath the German wire and jumped into their front-line trench.

Granddad never explained what happened to the Germans as he probably thought I'd have nightmares. However, he did tell me that when they jumped into a

German trench the Germans put up their hands and shouted '*Kamerad*' so they didn't shoot them but took them prisoner. Of course, the Germans got their own back when he was captured.

'What happened then?'

'I became a prisoner of war.'

I love Granddad's stories but soon they get shorter and often he is in bed.

Then for some reason the stories stop.

* * *

I can't wait for the Coronation but they say it will be at least a year. Before that our family has sad times. Mum calls it grieving. No one tells me what is happening with my grandad but one day in March 1952, Mum and Dad disappear and a neighbour comes to sit with me. When they come back, they tell me Granddad has passed away.

'That means he's dead,' Mum says seeing me look puzzled. Granny sniffs all the time and says, 'Oh dear, oh dear, oh dear.'

One day my parents dress up in dark clothes with black arm bands and the neighbour comes again. This time she brings some sweets and calls me 'duckie'. Another neighbour knocks the door and the first one says, 'No they aren't in, they're at the funeral.'

No sooner have they been to this funeral thingy than my family start looking worried about what is happening in the world. Mum and Granny talk about something called the BOMB.

'We've got the atomic bomb,' Granny says.
'It's the Cold War,' Mum says.
'Third nuclear power we are,' Dad sounds proud.

On the radio, the BBC people talk about it. Britain is now trying to build a bigger bomb.

'Space race,' the radio lady says.

'Waste of money!' Mum's usual rant.

'Why don't they rebuild the bomb sites instead,' Dad says. Some buildings are dangerous and have to be flattened. At the cinema, we see London's blown up houses on the Pathé News and children playing Cowboys and Indians chasing around rubble. It looks fun.

We don't see anything like it in Harpenden, but the boys up the road make go-karts. They use pieces of wood and wheels from old roller skates. They speed down the hill hitting the potholes and get shouted at by old ladies hobbling on the path with walking sticks. Mainly they play in the Spinney at the top of Grove Avenue.

* * *

Now I have to go to the Red House. I'm scared. My granddad came here. Look what happened to him! Anyway it seems I'll miss Harvest Festival this year and will be spared the embarrassment of walking into school with an armful of flowers and a bag of cabbages.

'You'll have ice cream after a sleep.' My mother is explaining what is to happen. Not only was I born in this red brick house but I have to go there to have my tonsils removed. It's the answer, apparently, to heavy colds and catarrh every winter. Say goodbye to bowls of steam with Friar's Balsam or Vick, breathing vapours with your head under a towel.

'We are going now.' My parents walk down the ward towards the door. After they leave, I shake with fear and a sick feeling invades my stomach. Is this homesickness? My sister has to go to boarding school because she's deaf. I wonder if this is how she feels when she goes back to school after a holiday. The men try talking to me and make jokes but I miss my parents so much I hide under the blankets and cry, stifling the noise so the men won't come to peep and see if I am OK.

The next day a nurse pricks my hand with a needle and then holds a horrid mask over my face. When I wake up I can't speak above a whisper. My mother visits. I cry and ask to go home. But, no, I have to stay until the doctor has seen my throat is healing which could be *MONTHS AWAY*.

In the evening my father comes in and I try to get round him. Usually I can get my own way with my dad but not this time.

* * *

Now it's 1952, tonsils are out and I'm left with only three grandparents – one is Granny who never stops talking, visiting all her sisters, brothers and in-laws every Sunday on her way to our house to glean the latest gossip. Then there is Batford Grandma, quiet and shy and a jolly, red-faced Granddad who laughs all the time.

'I can't stay on my own on a Sunday.' I hear Granny say this and see my mother's face fall at the prospect.

'You can come here for Sunday lunch, Mum.' My mother is giving in somewhat.

And later …

'Why does she have to come every week?' My father's face is cloudy.

Granny's Sunday visits show no signs of stopping even after she's got over Granddad's death.

Granny comes on Wednesday afternoons too, without even asking. When I see them talking though I detect that my mother likes her visits. It's my dad who doesn't.

'I've been to see Liz and then I went round to Alice.' Granny uses her visits to pop in to her sisters' houses. She collects all the family news. Liz is her sister at Hatching Green. She's married to Walter Freeman and has a son Jack who lives in Topstreet Way on Piggotshill Lane and a daughter, Bessie, whose husband, Jock, a Scot, insists the only way to eat porridge is sprinkled with salt.

'I'm just going up to see Sis.' Lunch is over. Granny is putting her coat on. Sis is her sister Sarah who lives at 27 Grove Avenue. She has a chicken field next to her bungalow.

'Do you want to come, Dinah?' If I go I can go into the chicken field and look for eggs. All the chicken houses have lift-up lids and I love looking for newly-laid eggs. Sometimes there's a brown egg which Auntie Sarah says is special.

'They taste better,' she reckons. Auntie Sarah and Uncle Arthur come for tea at Christmas, usually Boxing

Day. She's a rotund lady, a head cook in one of the big houses in Harpenden in the early 1900s. When I visit, she tosses me a jam tart. A gate in her garden leads to the field of chickens, clucking and scratching.

'Don't let them out,' Auntie Sarah shouts.

Eventually, my Uncle Charlie builds a bungalow on the chicken field. He married Jessie Pinney in the war and their son, Timothy, is eighteen months older than me. Our parents are friends. Before they married, the four of them holidayed together and the photo album is full of pictures of them having fun.

Sometimes Granny comes down to South Harpenden on the 321 bus. From there she might get off before the Skew Bridge and go to Queen's Road to see her sister-in-law, Eliza. Her older brother, Herbert, was gassed in the First World War and returned home a sick man only to die in 1920. Eliza has a daughter Agnes whose daughter Mollie is one of my oldest cousins although I don't meet her until 2013.

In good weather, Granny walks across Harpenden Common. From there she can walk up to Hatching Green or down to Queen's Road. Whatever the weather, she wears a hat. She has so many hats I never see her in the same one twice.

When Dad's shop is open, Granny can go to the shops by the short route, through a door from the rear room, where we keep our bikes, and which leads, through another door, to the foot of my grandmother's stairs. On these occasions she returns with a strange, furtive expression on her face, the contents of her bag chinking as she goes upstairs. My mother winks and jokes Granny has been stocking up on sherry.

'That's why she has a rosy complexion,' my mother says. It has nothing to do with fresh air and exercise although she does get plenty walking around Harpenden.

However, we don't have any relatives in the posher area further along the A6 known as West Common Way. A famous comedian does live there – Eric Morecambe, whose real name is Bartholomew. Mum loves to see Morecambe and Wise on television and she serves Mr and Mrs Bartholomew in Dad's shop.

Granny's brother, Tom, lives in Coleswood Road. He's a favourite brother as they are close in age. He has two sons, Ron and Frank. Ron and his wife are a double act and perform in pubs and at family weddings. Ron plays the piano and June sings. We visit them and their two daughters, Pat and Barbara. Frank, the younger brother, is an electrician and single. At family weddings and get-togethers Ron and June get a good singsong going.

All the Westons and Tuffins call my granny, Auntie Annie. Tuffin girls are beautiful. Granny's sister, Nell, lives in Cravells Road. She has about five children. Her first – a boy – died young. Her other children are Uncle Pete who has a smallholding near to Nomansland, Auntie Elsie who married Denis Turner in the war and Auntie Connie who is married to Jim Dines. There's another sister, Annie.

Beyond Auntie Sarah's bungalow, council houses have sprung up and more building is visible in the big post-war housing rush.

My parents speak nicely. My father is fussy about speech. He insists I don't call something a thingie or a thingamyjig.

'Everything has a proper name,' he says.
'What's the right time?' I ask.
'You mean the correct time?'

I never get it right. Or should that be correct?

June 1953 – The Coronation

We walk back across Harpenden Common, late. Well, it's late for me but I don't draw attention to it. Of course, I'm never allowed across the Common alone even in daytime; dire warnings of strange men resonate in my head. Tonight, there are the usual conversations between my parents about local gossip generally. As it's dark, we can only talk to my sister under a street lamp or if Dad shines his torch on our faces for her to lip-read.

I'm feeling cross. We can't watch the grand firework display as it's past my bedtime. Oh no! Wouldn't you think just this once … perhaps, on this very special occasion we could watch? My whining and moaning bring the usual peremptory 'give over' from my mother.

Susan tries to cheer me up. She says I looked very sweet when dressed up in the afternoon.

Sweet, my foot! I didn't want to be an acorn with a felt stalk sticking out of the top of my hat, nor would I choose, if asked, to have zigzag stiff net only just covering my bottom.

Of course, I don't win a Fancy Dress prize, disappointingly for my mother who prides herself on her dressmaking skills. She toiled on the costume, for at least a day, using scraps of material from the loft, working her Singer treadle machine until her legs ache. This is usually used for her make do and mend. She turns thin sheets sides to middle after which I have to wriggle in bed to avoid the seam. Frayed collars and cuffs on Dad's shirts are turned and socks are darned regularly. Even the darns are darned.

I wanted to go as a fairy but she can't afford the material! Anyway, it has to be to do with England or the Coronation.

Then there's a long lecture about the oak tree which I don't understand.

Anyway, in the end it's go as an acorn or nothing!

'Try to smile, Dinah,' Mum says as she takes my photograph. I am standing in the back garden, in front of Dad's rockery.

'Say cheese!'

Linda's mum dresses her as one of Cinderella's Ugly Sisters with lots of red lipstick and her hair is tied in an awful untidy bunch. She looks brilliant. Her mother offers for me to be the second ugly sister and my heart lifts briefly, but no. Mum says Cinderella doesn't fit the theme and insists on the acorn. After all it took all evening.

Then, later, after the long afternoon walk to Rothamsted Park, I am lined up with all the other seven-year-olds. Wow! How I envy them all. I see my friend is dressed as the Queen. Anything would be better than an acorn!

'Please, Dinah,' my mother pleads giving me a loving shove towards the line-up. 'Look happy.'

Me? How can I be happy? I'm stuck with knickers showing and a silly stalk sticking out of my hat.

So now here we are; the embarrassing fun activities over, we trudge past the funfair, the burly tanned men calling, 'Hi ya darlings,' walking home in the cold and the wet. Why can't we see the crowning of the Harpenden Coronation Queen?

Mum says, 'No.' and when she says no, that's it, even if I promise to eat my greens.

We are now past the Lower Common Ponds. The path nearby is boggy and I splatter mud up my legs.

Mum says, 'You are so messy, Dinah, why can't you walk properly?' I am! I am putting one foot in front of the other, aren't I?

'I am only seven!' I mutter. They forget that, my parents.

But… the best part of Coronation day for me, other than our surprise present, was having a day off school; a WHOLE DAY with no sums or spelling. Please don't let it end. I can't bear the idea of school the next day.

'At least you didn't have to stand all day in the rain,' my mother says, 'like all those people in London.'

I should think not. For the first time ever our family hasn't rushed off up to London for a big occasion. They've always been in the crowds lining the Mall for royal weddings and coronations. Any excuse and Mum and Granny Weston put on a silly hat and drag us to Harpenden station. Changing the Guard, Festival of Britain. You name it, we've done it. And we have to pose for photos too.

But today none of us stands in the rain. No wet hair, no shivering, no aching legs, no dripping coat. Today is different. That is why my granny is my favourite person. Isn't it she who gave us … the television?

We had begun the day as always listening to the BBC Home Service.

'Good morning listeners everywhere. It's seven o'clock on Tuesday the second of June and here is the news.'

We all have to be quiet while Dad listens.

'Can't we have the television on?' I get a curt 'no' from Mum. Apparently, we have to wait until later for the Outside Broadcast. So for now, nothing.

Suddenly the man, who always speaks on the radio, is talking about a mountain and Dad calls to Mum to tell her about it.

'Rennie,' he shouts up the stairs.

'They're up Everest.' He has stopped shaving at the sink. On cue, the paper boy arrives and the *Daily Express* drops through the letterbox. I run to pick it up wondering if there's a picture of the Princess Elizabeth. The papers have been full of pictures of her and Prince Philip for weeks. But, no, not today! There's a man's picture on the front page. He doesn't look like us and he has a funny name which I can't read. Dad says he comes from India and he looks like that because it's a hot country.

Granny Weston appears around eleven o'clock. Her television was brought home on Dad's bicycle the day before and put on a table in the corner of the dining room. It's just a box with a glass front and at first I can't see what the fuss is about. Granny went to Courtney Davis the electrical shop in Station Road. It's one of the first televisions in Harpenden. She bought it for herself but changed her mind, deciding we can have it instead.

It isn't just about the Coronation. There's another reason. My granny has given us the television, I realise, to guarantee a place in our living room whenever she wants, using the excuse there's a programme on television she wishes to watch. Wembley Cup Final, Trooping the Colour, the Olympics and some Saturday evenings she comes to our house to watch *Come Dancing*. I love that programme. The girls wear long, frilly, full dresses flying in the air as they swing round.

I think I'm the only one who sees through her generosity as Mum never says anything about it although I hear Dad moan after a few weeks.

'She's here again.'

Today, Dad has the day off work and he offers Mum and Granny a port or a sherry as a celebration. I wait, holding my breath, wondering if I'll be offered something.

'Do you want a port and lemon, Dinah?'

'Yes, please!' He doesn't need to ask. Of course, my sister and I are not drunks. It's all lemonade with a dash of colour out of the port bottle. We pretend it's what's drunk in pubs though.

'Where are you going to sit, Dinah?' They always ask that. I can only sit at the dining table. It's the only place left.

Granny and Mum have the two fireside chairs. Mum says it's cold enough to light a fire but Dad says you can't light a fire in June. So that's the end of that! Usually, Dad would do anything for Mum but not today apparently.

'Have you fed your rabbit, Dinah? Give Pam a special dinner eh?'

Anyone would think it was Christmas. I stay put. They'll forget when my sister asks what's happening.

Dad goes over to the little box and switches it on but nothing happens except for a small white light in the middle of the glass.

'Pull the curtains, Ken,' says Mum. 'Otherwise we can't see it.'

'You have to wait five or ten minutes for it to warm up,' says Granny. 'That's what they told me in Courtney Davis.'

We wait but nothing happens so Dad goes to the little box and fiddles with the switches and then, suddenly, there it is – well for a few minutes at least – a picture but it's sliding downwards so we can't see it properly. Then it starts sliding faster and faster, enough to make me feel dizzy. Anyway, Dad has luck with a switch at the back and we see it – a picture that stands still. There are sparkly crowns, long clothes on women, some horses with fluffy headdresses and soldiers with large hairy hoods. There are coaches like I see in picture books. As the screen appears to steady and the sound starts, Mum and Granny give Susan a running commentary.

'That's the Prime Minister of Australia.'

We can't see the man on the television who is talking. Anyway now he's describing the colours of the clothes that the Queen of Tonga is wearing.

Mum says, 'It's an island. We'll look it up later.'

I ask, 'What's that flashing light?'

Granny says, 'They're tiaras. They are glinting because they have diamonds on them.'

Granny has brought mince pies. I hate them but I say no thank you politely. I don't ask for anything else. I've seen a biscuit tin at Elsa's. It has the word BISCUITS on the lid.

Now the picture is fuzzy so Dad twiddles more knobs. Wow! A coach like Cinderella uses to go to the ball. The man says it's gold.

People are cheering and waving through the pouring rain. I can see they're holding umbrellas. Some people are soaked and their hair is plastered down their faces like when I have my hair washed.

Dad is still twiddling knobs and getting in the way, so we can't see. A loud whistle comes from the box.

'What's that?' Mum shouts.

'Nothing. It's just the set playing up. I don't think it likes being here in this corner. Perhaps I'll have to move the aerial.'

What I want to say is that the man who came to put up the big wire thingy on the chimney needed three ladders to get the large H wire shape on the roof but I think better of it as I can see an argument coming.

Now some neighbours come into our house to watch the actual crowning of our new Queen. Mum makes cups of tea and everyone says how lucky we are to have a television. Mrs Wallace from next door calls it a picture box. She keeps asking how the picture gets to our set in our living room.

There is silence.

Even Dad goes quiet and he usually knows everything No-one knows the answer.

But there's a problem. The picture comes and goes every time anyone walks in front of the set.

'Sit down,' says Dad.

All our neighbours are moving to see round my dad who's in the way twiddling knobs. I'm sure he made the television whistle. There's nothing to see except dots and wiggly lines.

'Ken, leave it! It's the rain, not the television.'

'What a shame,' says Granny. 'The most important day of her life and it rains.'

The cheering gets louder.

'Who's that?' asks Granny when we see a man getting out of a carriage.

I feel my father tense up. It happens when my granny is here.

'Listen, Mum, and you'll find out,' he says sharply. He is often irritated by Granny. She's the cross he bears for marrying my mum. I know because he told me once.

The room has descended into silence as we peer at fuzzy figures. Our excitement is fast disappearing. A strange feeling I later realise is disappointment sinks in my stomach.

But never mind. While we might feel slightly frustrated by the blurry lines and pictures sliding up and down, to us it's still a technical miracle. Not without its hitches, as Dad rightly says but through the fuzziness and the snowstorms, we see, in our own living room, diamonds, a golden coach and a queen being crowned.

Mum says, 'A new Elizabethan Age is here.' Not that I have a clue what she means. Still, no-one can take this day away from us. It will be forever stamped on our memory.

Later, our neighbours leave to go home, giving us kisses and hugs and thanking us for letting them see the moving pictures, and never mind they were fuzzy.

'Nearly home.' My mother is using her sing-song, let's be happy voice. We are near Crabtree Lane. We can hear fireworks. I'm disappointed I've missed them but can't say.

I am still wearing the acorn costume as we plod across Southdown Road and walk under the Skew Bridge and past the gas works. I can't wait to get my costume off. I will never, ever wear it again. I will lose it somehow. I can hide it, bury it.

What an embarrassing day. How can I say I enjoyed myself? After the awful experience in that stupid cap with a stalk on it, I'm even forced to wear it when we troop into the Public Hall for tea. I'm mortified.

'Can't I change?' I plead.

'No,' she says, 'just you go, enjoy yourself and, for goodness sake, stop scowling!'

Once inside the hall I see people I know. Oh dear, I think. Now everybody will know how stupid I look.

'What a lovely little acorn,' says the vicar's wife as she passes.

I can't believe what I see next. My friend is floating around in her Coronation costume, preening herself. The velvet train is identical to the one Princess Elizabeth wore, trailing across the floor. She has a crown on her head and a sash round her shoulders printed with the words FIRST PRIZE. When she sees me she waves and points to the book she's won. I'm seething; she doesn't even like reading, not like I do. It isn't fair. I plaster a pretend smile on my face to hide my jealousy. Why couldn't Mum make *me* a Coronation costume like that?

An acorn! I'll never live it down!

The Growth of the Media

Mum already listens to *Workers' Playtime*, *Mrs Dale's Diary* and *Woman's Hour* and the occasional play. She is a real radio fan.

I love *Uncle Mac's Children's Favourites* on Saturday mornings. He begins his programme, Hello, Children, everywhere. My favourites are 'Nellie the Elephant' and 'The Runaway Train'.

But the television is beginning to take over our lives. It's around 1954 that we see Roger Bannister run the four-minute mile on what Mum now calls the telly. She loves *The Grove Family* and *Fabian of the Yard*. I am already hooked on *The Flower Pot Men*, *Andy Pandy*, *Watch With Mother* and *Rag Tag and Bobtail*. My parents now discuss something they call politics when they watch *Panorama* and Mum sings lustily to *The Good Old Days* where people sit in Victorian dress and wave fans in front of their faces when it is hot. They call out and heckle the compere.

One day Dad brings home a new radio and tells me I can have the old one in my bedroom. He carries it upstairs and puts it on the dressing table leaving just enough room for my Pond's vanishing cream. From that day, I begin a love affair with the *Light Programme* enjoying *Take it from Here*, written by Frank Muir and Denis Norden and starring Jimmy Edwards. On Sunday lunchtime Jean Metcalfe broadcasts two-way family favourites for families and servicemen overseas.

Television in 1953 was only black and white and the sets take five minutes to warm up, irritating if your favourite programme is imminent. It is also necessary to pull the curtains if you want to see a clear picture so the living rooms of Harpenden were curtained off during daily broadcasting. At first, there were only approximately three hours a day of broadcasting.

Commercial television with the adverts for items such as toothpaste and deodorant was not launched until 22 September 1955 when Independent Television (ITV) began broadcasting. We sing 'Murray mints, Murray mints, too good to hurry mints.'

And my dad would sing 'you'll wonder where the yellow went when you brush your teeth with Pepsodent.'

The PG Tips advert with the chimpanzees was a favourite but was stopped in the 1970s when animal rights activists complained. It returned in 2002.

A popular 1950s advertisement on Independent Television broadcasts was Katie advertising Oxo cubes as having 'man appeal'. Advertisements reinforced the stereotype with pictures of women knitting, her children at her feet and having a meal waiting for her husband when he came home from work.

My mother fits the 1950s stereotype. She exchanges tips with neighbours over the garden fences on tasty dishes recipes or how to clean certain items. There was no shortage of information as women in the fifties prided themselves on good homemaking skills on a budget. Women's magazines featured domesticity and little else except how to be a good housewife, cleaning rooms on certain days of the week without fail regardless of home emergencies, sickness or other mishaps.

On television, there are frequent breaks in transmission with signs reading 'Normal service will be resumed as soon as possible' and interludes because slick programme timing was yet to take off. Music and repetitive films kept us amused such as *The Potter's Wheel*, *The Spinning Wheel*, *The White Kitten*, *Angel fish*, *Horses* (ploughing a field), and of course the classic *London to Brighton in 4 Minutes*.

Long periods showed a test card. Transmission breakdowns were common. Television announcers sat at desks and introduced each programme. Celebrities included Sylvia Peters, Peter Haigh, McDonald Hobley, Mary Malcolm, Robert Dougal and Valerie Pitts. Sylvia Peters also fronted BBC Children's *TV For Deaf Children* in 1956 and Susan and I watch together when she's home.

Sylvia Peters, a former musical actress, joined the BBC in 1947 after answering a newspaper advertisement for a continuity announcer and was one of the post-war trio of announcers who stayed until 1958. She also presented BBC TV's *Come Dancing* between 1954 and 1958.

For my sister and me, the excitement of television was never forgotten. Even black and white was luxury and presenters spoke what my mother called BBC! Others referred to presenters having a plum in their mouth, later 'talking plummy'.

Soon we were not the only people with a television. By the end of the fifties decade there were 10 million television sets in Britain.

Another favourite, *Muffin the Mule*, a string puppet, trotted around the top of a piano played by Annette Mills, sister of actor, John Mills. Made in 1934 by Fred Tickner, maker of the Hogarth puppets including Punch and Judy, Muffin used his very large head in conversations with Annette. Muffin was worked by Anne Hogarth standing on the piano behind a screen, invisible to us. This lovable puppet last appeared in 1955 days before Annette Mills died.

Another favourite, the marionette, Andy Pandy, came into my living room soon after our television arrived although he'd been on television since 11th July 1950. Another string puppet, he portrayed a chubby fresh-faced toddler in a bedtime outfit. He and his two friends Teddy and Looby Lou, a rag doll, lived in a picnic basket. Only twenty-six original black and white episodes were made, these seen time and again to unwary pre-school-age children.

These programmes featured on *'For the Children'*, later *'Watch with Mother'*. A further addition was *Flower Pot Men* (Bill and Ben) in 1952, made out of flowerpots, their hands large gardening gloves, their feet hobnailed boots.

Bill and Ben were puppet stars of 1950s and 1960s children's television. They lived in flower pots behind the potting shed and spoke their own language, Oddle Poddle largely made up of 'flibadob' and 'flobadob'. Criticised for promoting immaturity, the programme, however, became a classic.

Autumn 1953

I run as fast as my chunky legs can carry me, my hand-knitted socks trickling down my calves, my scabby knee bleeding and open to the elements. Half the garter from one sock now hangs from a thorny branch. I gulp with fear that I've left evidence of my presence. I gather speed until I gasp for breath and my throat burns. My British Home Stores school blouse sticks to my skin and sweat dribbles down my face like a dripping tap.

With my back to the house I am still fleeing as I brace myself for the hole in the prickly hedge where I scratched my legs going in five minutes before. The Apple man mustn't see my face. I must escape or risk a line-up in assembly. The thought of an identity parade keeps me running.

In seconds my legs sting and I have more gouged skin. I smell blood as the pain sears through my body. My right hand tries to protect me from the thorns. I glance as blood oozes through my nail-bitten fingers.

The exposed left garter, now tight, pinches my skin. I wrench my tunic from the prickles, my stomach sinking at the sight of hanging threads. My gabardine mackintosh is flapping open and Mum's hand knitting hasn't fared too well either.

I don't know who scares me most, the Apple man or the boy who goaded me into stealing apples. It's his fault – he can't have checked the coast was clear. His jeering and pushing led to this but what do I have to show for it? Nothing. I've made a schmuck of scrumping and now I am going to pay for it.

'I'll get you kids one day, just you wait and see. I'll have your guts for garters.'

Well, I think, my guts are spewing down to my garters so I don't have much to lose, do I? And there's more. Too late I smell pee.

* * *

My parents are firm but they aren't strict. I've rarely had a slap. It wouldn't occur to them to use corporal punishment, unlike teachers with a cane or slipper taken from the cupboard and administered without a second thought. Miss Hairy Legs piles on the agony and humiliation for those – usually boys – who don't follow her prescribed path. The offender is sent to the cupboard to collect the instrument of torture, extending the terrifying anticipation of the stinging whack. Then, more quivering delay while she reports in her clipped Scottish accent the scale of his misdemeanour, swinging Joey, the slipper, back and forth in front of her victim as his petrified face reddens with embarrassment. It's to be a lesson to us all. She doesn't waste a whacking. We all must feel it and sense the dread so we learn through fear.

Her sharp eyes search the room and settle wide-eyed and witchlike on other would-be wrongdoers as she spits out the number of whacks the shivering wreck is to receive before finally saying those most dreaded words.

'Touch your toes.'

I am never sent to get Joey, my one aim at Manland Junior School to get through to the eleven-plus without receiving that or the cane but how I escape I cannot fathom. Often the ringleader at playtime or in class, I chivvy others to dastardly acts for which the penalty of discovery is the swish of a fast-moving piece of bamboo.

Some teachers use a ruler, some hit round the head, giving stinging slaps that make the recipient bounce off his chair.

'If ever,' Mum says, 'you are hit on the head, you tell me and there will be hell to pay. I'll be down that school like a dose of salts.'

She has one deaf daughter and so she doesn't want another one. One blow can deafen a child, she says.

Jimmy is an example of a glutton for punishment. He never learns. He has the thinnest trousers – so worn, his skin gleams through the cloth. When he gets the slipper it sounds as if it's whacking on bare skin. Mum says he's dressed from the charity people and jumble sales.

'It's not his fault,' she says kindly before pursing her lips. 'His parents are divorced.'

'What's that?' I ask. I've never heard the word.

As we get on the bus, Mum lowers her tone. 'His father ran off.'

'So he hasn't got a dad?' I ask.

'Somewhere in America, I think.' Mum is whispering now. She'd hate to be called a gossip, even though she is.

On Monday I take a long look at Jimmy. I don't know any other boy who has no dad. There's Wendy of course.

'That's different,' says Mum. 'Her father was killed at Arnhem.'

Mum's face changes and shows sadness. She sees me looking curious.

'It's what happened in the war,' she says.

After school finishes, I walk up Sauncey Avenue, muttering to myself some fancy lines for my latest written masterpiece. I'm always writing stories despite my mother's disdain. Normally, I turn left into Carlton Road and walk past the Red House where I was born and then to my dad's shoe repair shop in Station Road. Behind the workshop my bike awaits. My great-uncle owns the business and I love him. Everyone needs an uncle like him. His face lights up when I bounce through the door. I jabber about my day and enjoy a cup of tea before cycling the one and a half miles home to Southdown. Only today they won't be graced with my presence.

Every morning, I trudge the two miles to Manland School from Dad's shop in all weathers, panting as my little legs try to move faster, ignoring the squelching shoes and dripping clothes in fear of a slapped leg or lost playtime if I am late. At such times I hear in my mind the swish of the cane and the hard clap of a slipper on a boy's backside and pray it will never be me. At the end of the day, I am often cold and wet as I make the bell tinkle on the door of the shop.

Today, though, I am more terrified my mother's slim five-foot figure will appear in Thomson's Close. It's warm so she'll be wearing her blue and white floral shirt-waister with her navy cardigan. She's taking me to the ogre that is our dentist, an even more terrifying experience. If I could avoid it I would. Nothing endears me to the white-coated Mr Smiley Face as he singles me out for fillings and leaves my sister crowing with pleasure.

'Sweets,' he said on my last visit. 'You eat too many; it ruins the teeth.'

I pretend not to hear but he makes sure I do. On one of the two seats by the surgery door Mum sits bolt upright clasping her hands tightly together and fiddling nervously with the button on her boucle coat, her flesh-coloured stockings puckered and gathered at the knee where her legs are tightly crossed. Her face glows bright red.

'Such an embarrassment,' she says.

The dentist beckons and my heart sinks into my navy knickers at the thought!

My sister is slumped on the seat alongside, eager for her turn. I sit swallowed up by the large chair, gripping the sides until my fingers hurt. I moan as the dentist moves forward.

'I am nowhere near you, Dinah,' he says.

Soon I hear the familiar gurgling noises coming from my throat as the dreaded drill buzzes, vibrates and grinds into my teeth. If I make enough noise, I reckon, they might think I am choking, even … dying? But neither my mother nor my sister cast as much as one sympathetic glance in my direction.

'You should be at boarding school,' says my grandmother later, nodding knowingly in her 'I know I am right' fashion. Mum must have got that smug expression from her. No sweets allowed, no sugar on puddings and Matron stands over them to make sure they clean their teeth properly night and morning. Granny's lip curls with pleasure enjoying my discomfort.

Trust my Granny Weston to bring that up. She won't listen. Mum says my amalgam-filled holes are the result of rationing and her poor wartime diet.

'No-one was fat in the war,' she says. 'You were lucky to survive, your sister and you.'

I am still running when I glimpse my mother's red hair escaping her headscarf and flying in the wind as she pedals her bicycle with ease down the Close. I take a deep breath and look back but the Apple man has disappeared. The bully has also vanished, unwilling to wait around once he heard the Apple man shout. The apples I pinched have long since dropped from my scratched hands and, by the time my mother reaches me, I have no evidence on me of my recent misdemeanours. So I think.

'What's wrong? You're all red in the face.'

'Am I?' I feign surprise. 'I was running.'

Mum's sharp look makes me flinch. 'Running? What were you doing?' She isn't daft and knows when I am hiding something. Ever suspicious, her eyes scan me from head to foot then settle on my grazes.

'How did you get these?' Her touch makes me wince.

'I fell over.'

'And why were you running?'

'I was late getting out of school.'

'Late? Were you kept in? What had you done?'

'Nothing,' I say. My brain is working overtime. Ah. 'I lost my coat.'

'Your coat? How can you lose a coat at school? Don't you have pegs?'

'Yes, it fell off the peg.' I am getting sick of the charade and am about to own up to apple scrumping. It seems preferable to a half-cocked excuse about a dropped coat but fate is on my side when Mum sees someone she knows. Her face changes to a broad smile as she greets one of my many relatives. Or a friend? I am not sure which. Mum and Dad know everyone in Harpenden and, when I say everyone, I mean every person we meet.

'Hello, Rène. How's Ken. How's Susan?' If we are related or she knows them from school they call her Rène but, if they are workmates from Green's in St Albans, they call her Ginge. If I mention someone at school, she usually says she knows their parents from the Board School, Vaughan Road, the Public Hall dances where she met my father or as customers of her father's grocery shop. There are other links; The Red House is one.

While meeting Auntie M saves me from an inquisition, I soon realise we will be late. My mother never stops talking. Auntie Maureen is pretty and she doesn't ride a bicycle as she likes high heels and tight skirts. She teeters alongside Mum's bike as we walk up the Close towards Sun Lane Bridge.

'I remember you being born,' says Auntie Maureen. Here we go again, I think. More going over old times.

'When's your birthday again, Dinah?' Auntie M isn't that close a relation that she remembers this.

'September.'

'Yes, I remember now. So much going on.' Auntie M disappears down Thomson's Close.

'What was going on?' I watch her totter down the path.

'It was the end of the war and they'd dropped the atom bomb on Hiroshima and Nagasaki so before we knew where we were it was VJ Day.'

I know what VJ means. My father talks about the war, Hitler, the A bomb on Japan.

'Yes, Victory in Japan. Just before you were born. They surrendered.'

'Did you go dancing?' She shakes her head. Apparently she was in hospital getting over it when everyone else was out tripping about, laughing and singing. I think 'it' means the war. Later … much later … I discover 'it' means childbirth.

But now there are more important things, like the dentist.

My heart sinks as my mother wrinkles her nose and sniffs.

'What's that smell?'

I shrug and try to change the subject but she's having none of it. Her face moves nearer. I have to think quickly.

'I fell in something, I think.'

'What?'

'I dunno. Might be dog's stuff.'

'Oh well, can't be helped.'

With that Mum sits me on her bicycle saddle and I pray she won't touch me down there and realise I've wet myself. I have to remember to get a flannel and wash her seat down before she uses her bike again and recognises that familiar smell. But for now we have other things on our minds. Mum begins pushing me further up Thompson's Close to Carlton Road where we cross the road and go over the bridge above the railway track. I hear the familiar hoot of a train as it approaches, so we wait for it to pass under the bridge enveloping us in white steam. It leaves us coughing and spluttering as the smoke chokes us and stings our eyes till they run with tears. Then, as always, I run to the other side of the road to see the train come out the other side of the bridge. I wave to the driver who is hanging out of his door, looking up at me and waving back through the white mist. He whistles at my mum and her face goes red.

Once the train disappears in the murky distance chugging along on its way to London, we head down Sun Lane emerging in the lower High Street opposite the Cock Public House. We turn right and Mum trudges past the blacksmith's forge and a little further on where I can see the Glen Eagle Hotel hiding behind the trees. A man in a dark suit and carrying a black case is parking a car and walking towards the entrance.

'Who stays there?' I ask.

'Businessmen. Not people like us. It's for posh folks.'

As we near the Embassy Cinema I try reading the writing on a poster outside. I remember seeing the film of the Coronation there and recently Mum has taken me to see war films.

'What's on?' I ask.

'Never you mind! We're not here for the cinema, we need to sort that tooth out.'

This is an extra appointment. Three visits a year are three too many for me, although I'd prefer none or if I really have to go ... just one. We always go to the dentist in the school holidays which ruins the anticipation of the freedom from school, but, when I moan, my mother insists it's my behaviour that ruins it for her. Now Mum makes us go on the first day of the holidays.

'To get it over with,' she says.

Of course for this trip we could take the 321 bus from the Cock to Douglas Road. But, no. Mum has brought her bike.

Also we are early so Mum says, chirpily as always, 'That's what the Lord gave you legs for.'

This always means a long walk and I don't make a fuss. Mum stands no nonsense such as moaning about tired legs. Really, I suspect she wants to save the bus fare. Actually, I want to say, I'd rather put up with the toothache than go to Douglas Road to see the dentist.

Mum sees my face as we turn the corner and she pounces like a cat.

'All that fuss you made last night about a sore mouth. Don't now tell me you don't want to go.'

I reach for the big brass handle on the large front door and turn it and the mere smell of the dentist's hallway sends my heart rushing down to my boots and I feel tight collywobbles in my tummy. Once inside, I sit in the high chair as the drill starts finding its way into my fillings. I am ready to start my choking act which usually makes him stop. But, I get a nice surprise!

Phew! Today there's nothing to be done. It's just a new tooth pushing its way into view. Mr Schofield's nose twitches and he seems in a hurry to get away from me. I am elated so I really don't care. Once outside I jump on to Mum's bicycle again, sitting on her saddle and holding my breath still in the hope that she won't sniff. As we turn on to the main road and pass the bus stop, one of the Manland teachers cycles up the Luton Road past Douglas Road. She nods in my direction and pedals on.

'Who's that?' Mum asks and I tell her.

'She must live in Kinsbourne Green,' Mum says.

* * *

'Was that your sister?' The teacher asks the next morning. She knows I have a sister who doesn't come to my school.

'Fancy,' I think, 'Mrs A thinking Mum is my sister.' When I tell my mother, her face first creases into a smile and then she laughs out loud, beaming with utter pleasure. She's vain especially with her auburn locks and tiny waist. She knows she looks younger than her years – many people tell her – and she loves every minute of it.

* * *

I am sitting in class at school. I don't know what age I am – perhaps six or seven – and the teacher's name intermittently used in the never-ending day that is Monday, is forgotten.

I can hear the rustle of paper around me and some whispering so it cannot be a test. I feel the small hard wooden chair cutting into my skin and leaving imprints of the slats at the tops of my thighs.

The rustling increases along with squeaks as chairs are moved just enough to make the occupant's fidgeting apparent. I can taste wood from chewing into my pencil and white pieces of splinters stick between my teeth which I pick at. The taste mingles with the lunchtime custard, so typical of school dinners it seems an eternity it has been there – forever.

I hear the teacher talking, allowing one person to go to the toilet, another classmate to fetch a rubber to erase something he has written incorrectly. What about me? I want to shout. How can I finish my story with all this noise but when I look up all I can see are my classmates with hunched shoulders, poring over their work. There's Mary, the swot whose work will be perfect and David, who always gets top marks, followed by Christopher, who always knows the date because his father shows him the newspaper every morning.

My parents don't let me near the paper except to see the Gambols cartoon on the back of the *Daily Express*. They say it's full of trouble in the world. But, whatever they think, I am sure Christopher's family don't take the *Express*. He's never heard of the Gambols, he said.

Soon our teacher will tell us it's playtime but there's no clock in the room so I think she must wear a watch. Strange, I have never seen her wearing it before today. But here I see it as her hand passes across the table to remove a finished piece of work. The watch is small and dainty but I cannot read it so I keep my head down to make the most of the last few minutes of the lesson.

Perhaps this time I will finish my story or perhaps I can ask, as I did last week, to stay in during playtime to finish it.

The Common – 1951

'You're not going in.' Mum is standing behind me at the Silver Cup Pond as I near the edge. I'm desperate. I want to put my toe in. I take off the Clark's sandals but my mother grabs the full skirt of my dress to stop me falling into the water. In the sunlight, the dull grey of the water contrasts with the bright green grass. Children run in and out of the water. Some boys sail their boats. One rich boy has a boat he controls with a box in his hand. Mum says it has something called a battery.

We've walked across the Common and we're heading for the Village. We took the dusty path opposite Crabtree Lane through trees and bushes and across the grass. The pub opposite the pond is The Silver Cup. Ahead are the Baa Lamb trees and to the right the road leads to the lower road and the Friends' Meeting House. I'm hoping we're off to the Public Hall but I forget it's summer, so no bazaars.

'You can get polio from dirty water.' Mum again. I don't know if it's true but take her word for it.

Mum is talking to someone. I hear her say The Bowling Alley and Weston's grocery. I recognise the woman from Smith's in the High Street where I go after Christmas with money to buy a book.

That's where my mother grew up. The Bowling Alley; the area of Southdown between Skew Bridge and Piggotshill Lane. Some people think Southdown is poor. Mum was born in Coleswood Road where Granny lived with her sister-in-law while my Granddad was away in the First World War.

Granny's father, Arthur Tuffin, had arrived in Harpenden in 1868, met and married Lizzie Parrot three years later. They had eight children, her eighth being Granny but sadly Lizzie died a month later. Lizzie's mother then moved in to look after the children.

Within a year, Arthur had married Harriet who started her own family – five children on top of the eight already in the family. Often, the stepmother expected baby Annie, my grandmother, to help out with the half siblings and her life was not easy.

By the time my grandfather returned from the war my mother was three years old with a tousled mass of auburn hair and freckled skin sensitive to the sun's summer rays. It was Granddad's wish she was named Rène possibly a name he encountered in France. One possibility is it was a shortened form of Irene. In fact, when Mum was twelve years old, Miss Emerton, her teacher, used the name Irene in my mother's autograph book.

My grandparents both wrote memorable, thought-provoking entries in this autograph book. My grandmother wrote 'Listen much, speak little; say nothing you may be sorry for. Take care of your spare moments, they are the gold dust'.

Despite my grandmother's short education – she left school at twelve – the handwriting is neat and there are no spelling mistakes. My grandfather's wise entry, 'Keep your face to the sun and the shadows will fall behind you', was similarly well-written. My grandparents were the first members of their families to benefit from the 1870 Education Act although, coming from large poor families, they both left school at twelve years old.

As Granny's older sisters settled in marriage or in service, Annie went to live with them in turn rather than stay with her stepmother. Eventually, her older sister, Sarah, obtained a position for her as kitchen maid at the house where she worked as Cook. In 1902 girls from poorer backgrounds tended to work in service until they married and had children themselves.

1951

I have to wear a crisply ironed starched dress. The hard material of the hem scratches my legs. Even scratchier is the smocking, the gathered material with embroidery stitches. Up and down on my flat nipples.

'Smocking is babyish,' I say. 'I am six years old, don't you know.' The skirt of the dress sticks out at the back and it's too short. I hate it.

Today we visit Auntie Alice, Granddad Weston's sister. She helped the nurse when my mum burst into the world in 1916. Granny lived with her. It was wartime. Not the one my dad was in but the one before. They said it was the war to end all wars but it wasn't. Dad says all politicians lie.

'I need a coat,' I say getting my gabardine mac from the downstairs cloakroom.

'You don't,' Mum says. 'We're late.'

I want the coat to hide the dress. It's a hand-down. I have my sister's old clothes and some from my second cousins. Some are so nice, I can't wait to grow big enough to wear them. But not this one.

It only takes five minutes to walk down Grove Avenue, along Grove Road, past my Uncle Reg's house and turn left.

Uncle Reg and Auntie Rose have no children. They did have a little girl, Betty, who was bridesmaid at Mum and Dad's wedding. Soon after, she ran into the road and was hit by a car and killed. She was their only child and Mum always bought anemones for them at Christmas like those in Betty's bouquet.

Auntie Alice lives in Coleswood Road in a house called Alma Cottage, so I look for the nameplate. I know she has a son called Bob.

'He's manager now.'

'That's good,' says my mother.

She's peering at some new photographs on Auntie's dresser.

We call Auntie Alice's son Uncle Bob but he's Mum's cousin. He worked in a bank before the war and signed up for the Royal Air Force after September 1939. He was shot down when out on a mission and spent the rest of the war as a prisoner of war. The Red Cross sent study materials and arranged his banking exams.

My Granddad, Bertie Weston, left school at thirteen and worked at one of the village grocery stores as an assistant and delivery boy. On his return from France in 1919, he opened Weston's grocer's shop at 102 Southdown Road next to the Oggelsby garage at the foot of Walker's Road. It's in the spacious first and second floor rooms that my mother grows up.

At the side of the shop, a passageway leads to their rear garden, with an Anderson shelter, and other back gardens belonging to Providence Place, a row of cottages facing the Triangle, the green separating Walkers Road from Southdown Road. In one cottage live the Pearce family. Nan and my mother are childhood friends.

According to Granny, my parents began courting when my mum was sixteen and my father eighteen. But, on Sunday 3rd September 1939, when they are twenty-six and twenty-three respectively, war was declared on Germany and the love-birds, as she calls them, wanted to tie the knot.

Mum and Dad eventually make the dash up the aisle on Boxing Day. Granny Weston is not that happy about the timing – her only daughter after all. There are no caterers left in Harpenden – they've all been called up – so she spends Christmas Day preparing food. Few men remained available for the heavier work such as setting up tables in the local church hall. Many already had their places taken by evacuees at the dinner tables of Harpenden. It was, therefore, left to my Granny Weston to cater for the very large families of the Munts, Smiths, Westons and Tuffins just when bombs were expected to fall at any minute. On top of that, she has to tape over their windows in case bombs drop and shatter the glass.

* * *

Mum loved her first home in Wheathampstead. The Smith family were builders and Dad heard a house in Lea Valley was up for rent in 1939. They don't live there long.

Soon after, my father gets his call up and is posted far away but just close enough to come home on forty-eight-hour leaves. His ID papers show a forty-eight-hour pass every week but there were about five occasions with NO in the column. In 1941, when my sister was born, there were a few marked YES. Once he passed his exams with flying colours and was quickly promoted to instructor. He stayed in England marching young boys up and down the camp parade grounds and didn't see active service.

The day after Dad left, my grandmother persuaded Mum to move back to Southdown. She then sublet the house for the duration of the war.

By mid-1940, still expecting invasion, my mum is pregnant and my sister is born in 1941. At six months old, Susan contracts meningitis which leaves her profoundly deaf. Mum's friend, Nan, already has a baby girl, Wendy, and the two mothers spend happy times together. The little girls play contentedly, the divide between the Deaf and hearing seemingly overcome with little difficulty.

After D-Day, without more raw recruits, my father is deployed to the Military Police and sent to France. His job was to keep law and order. He learnt to drive and sometimes rode a motorbike.

'I saw people, just like you and me,' he says, 'crawling out of cellars, sewers and holes in the ground where they'd been hiding from the fighting. They were scavenging in the dustbins and looting shops. All of them starving.'

During her pregnancy, my mother worked at de

Havilland Aircraft in Hatfield issuing spare parts for Mosquito aircraft. She left two months before I was born.

Amidst the jubilation after VJ (Victory over Japan) Day in August 1945, my mother goes into hospital to reduce her blood pressure. Rest is not forthcoming as I make my appearance two weeks early in the Red House. By then it's a mid-September and I weigh 5 pounds 12 ounces.

So what's in a name? Mum's choice of a name for me causes confusion and not just at school. Why Dinah?

She herself had been given an unusual name so she should have known better. My name is never pronounced properly. I am Deena, Diane, Diana, whereas Mum's name – Renè – had only one variation which was 'Rennie', given to her by my father.

'That's a funny name,' says a classmate and I cringe.

'It's in the Bible,' insists Mum. She's C of E and proud of it. There's no escape through abbreviation either. In fact, if friends shorten my name I face her wrath. Likewise my sister is never Sue.

In the maternity ward, Mum meets Mrs Bangle whose son, Alan, is in my class at Manland.

For now though, with Dad still away, Mum lives at 102 Southdown Road so it's there I am taken from hospital, jiggled about by two evacuees (who are reluctant to return to London), my sister in her school holidays and two doting grandparents. My father hitchhikes from his base and enjoys a brief compassionate leave. Now in England, he has to wait for his demob. Hitching a lift on the back of a motorbike on 4th November 1945 he sees me baptised. The parish magazine also lists the christening of Derek Robert Prichard on the 3rd. Derek, like Alan, is a future classmate.

Advertisements in the parish magazine that October reflect the character of the Bowling Alley in late 1945; there's the boast of personal service by Coleswood Stores, near Auntie Alice's house, and BEST BREAD AND CAKES from Rowe and Sons, advertised as 'obtainable under present conditions', which Mum says means rationing.

Mum tells me how lucky we are. Many men returning from the war find there are no jobs and some sweethearts have new boyfriends. Some have fallen for Yanks and have babies. Others even go to America.

This doesn't happen to us. My parents are always kissing and cuddling. Also, fortunately for us, Uncle Charlie kept my father's job for him – a promise made in 1939.

Within weeks of my dad coming home the tenants at 45 Manor Road are despatched and we move back to Wheathampstead where we spend four happy years.

Dad now cycles from Lea Valley to Station Road and home for lunch each day, his trousers fastened with clips to keep the trouser legs free from the oily chain.

Of course, at nine months old I don't remember or understand any of this and I am busy with my own problems. I've caught whooping cough. Trying to get your breath causes a whoop. Before the illness I am crawling but I go back to being a floppy baby. Many children died as inoculations weren't introduced until the 1950s.

Mum pushes me proudly around Wheathampstead and Harpenden in a large Silver Cross carriage pram. When my sister is home, she sits in the bottom of the pram and Mum pushes us both up to Harpenden Village or Southdown to see our grandparents. In the war the main area of the Silver Cross factory was used by the Air Ministry for producing airplane parts. Afterwards, the company applies the techniques developed manufacturing warplanes to develop new prams. They replace plywood bodies with aluminium and quickly produce the finest baby products. Even the Queen chooses Silver Cross for Prince Charles in 1948. However, in 1945, restricted production is still in force so I am paraded in a pram handed down from a neighbour or relative. Babies then are put outside in all weathers.

Mum baths me in the sink or in a bowl on the kitchen table wearing a waterproof apron, a towel across her lap. First, wrapped up in a towel and held over the bath for a hair wash. After rubbing it dry, the mother soaps the baby on her lap and then lowers the baby into the water. My mother uses her elbow to test the water temperature. After wrapping me in a warmed towel, I'm dried and powdered; powder soon discontinued for health reasons. I suffer no asthma or chest problems from a frequent dousing of talc. Zinc and castor oil cream is used to prevent or treat nappy rash. Nappies are terry towelling or muslin, folded into a triangle and fastened with large nappy pins in the front. Soiled nappies are soaked in cold water, boiled either in a large cauldron on the cooker or the fire and, if a family can afford it, a special boiler to keep the nappies white.

Dad wasn't used to young babies, Mum said. Away in the army when Susan was born and waiting to be demobbed when I arrive. His sleep is never disturbed except when on leave. Returning soldiers, sailors and airmen aren't used to babies and young children. 1950s fathers don't change nappies, help with potty training or deal with toddlers. However, our father uses his talents to make toys. He's good at picnics, brewing up on a primus stove and, when we are older, takes us on long cycle rides.

But he loved pushing the pram. Dad makes Mum laugh with his silly jokes. A modest, shy man, he only reacts if someone puts him down. I'm reared to be proud of my roots. I never hear rows or arguments.

Once back in Lea Valley, we see more of the Munt family. My father's brother, Hector, is six years younger and, after the war, he courts a Batford girl, Betty Bent. Sometimes they walk from Batford Road to Manor Road to visit on a Sunday afternoon. There is no bathroom in either my grandparents' house or at Betty's home; both families use tin baths in front of the fire and privacy is lacking. So the bathroom at number 45 is used on their visits!

1949

I am often asked, 'Do you remember moving here?'

Nope. Well I do remember a few things. Mud, no grass, no hedges, no flowers, newspaper on the kitchen floor, Pam's hutch stuck at an angle about to tip over. I remember later helping Dad mix cement.

'Hold tight,' he says and I do. I never fall. I grip the handlebars with one hand and the crossbar with the other. The metal is cold on my bare buttocks where my knickers have risen above what they are meant to hide. Precariously perched aloft, I look down on the world I know – a small world of shopkeepers, coal fires, cold bathrooms, tin baths, rides on the crossbar, bus rides to Auntie Mac …

… and, when I am lifted down, I feel the indents on my skin from the crossbar.

'You stay with Granny.' Dad stops at the Triangle opposite Granddad's shop. But I don't want to. I want to see the new house. I'm worrying about my rabbit. I last saw her looking dolefully out through her hutch mesh as Mr Spacey shut the removal van.

Auntie Mac (Cissy) is Uncle Charlie's sister and my mother's cousins. Cissy marries a policeman, Ron Matravers, and lives in Colne Avenue, Rickmansworth which they call Ricky. We call them Auntie and Uncle Mac although perhaps she should be Auntie Mat. Uncle Charlie Hawkins is called Son by all the family including Mum and Dad. My family is full of nicknames or short names. Mum is Rennie, Dad is Ken. My Granny Weston calls her sister Sarah, Sis, and her husband is Bert. I want to ask why I don't have a nickname.

I have a seat on the back of Mum's bike and I hold on tight to the sides. I mustn't fall but sometimes I wonder …

'I have enough to do without any accidents from you.' It would be inconvenient. I must hold on.

At the house, Dad beams with pride as he surveys his acquisition. He moves around the kitchen/diner touching the walls and the wooden worktop. He peers into the white enamel sink, turns on a tap and watches the water swirl around the plughole. He says, 'Look at this,' and, 'look at that.' I hear the thrill in his voice. He's waited for years.

'Even before I married your mum,' he says excitedly, 'I wanted my own house. Even as a young boy. All the Munts and Smiths own houses.' I hear Mum murmur about her family of Tuffins and Westons. Yes, they too. We are a family of home owners.

I know Smith's builders built the house. I also know that Grandma Munt was a Smith before she married Granddad Munt. Her father gave her a wedding present of two houses – one to live in and one to rent out for income. Such is the value of property ownership in our family.

Dad bought the land before the war. Once demobbed, he makes plans but post-war building restrictions add further delay, so we wait until 1949 to take possession.

But some things have changed. My dad remembers

1938 when fields sat above the plot, but now council houses have sprung up. Dad can't get a mortgage or put in plans because of post-war restrictions but that doesn't stop the council putting up houses for their tenants. The project takes so long he's barely noticed these other houses being built.

When my parents take a walk they find the council houses are larger than their modest self-build. But, worse, their road has tarmac while our part of the road doesn't.

'A new road,' Dad sighs.

'What's the difference,' I ask. Our road isn't adopted apparently. It's private.

Mum can't hide her disappointment. She didn't understand the drawings, although Dad tried to explain. He gave her sizes and drew pictures but they meant nothing. I'm sympathetic as I am no Gauguin either. While Mum is eventually happy there, she confides to me it's not her desired layout. My father would be hurt if he found out. The trouble is she will always love Lea Valley more than Grove Avenue.

But some things are better. At Grove Avenue, the milk is delivered in glass bottles sealed by cardboard tops. We use these cardboard tops to make pom-poms – balls made by winding wool round two cardboard circular bottle tops through the hole in the middle and round the outside; all spare wool is used up this way and the more colours there are, the better the effect. Once you can't push any more wool through the hole, you tie a knot and put wool round it close to the base and tie it to fasten the centre of the strands. Then we cut the wool at the outside edge after which the wool falls into a wonderful woolly pom-pom.

Sadly, the newer foil tops can't be recycled in this way, a great pity. However, there's a greater novelty.

On waking, I listen for the milkman. No motor noise but the clip clop of Dolly the horse; Mr Watler and his milk cart. Some crates hold full bottles of milk and others sit smeared and empty. Mum is fussy washing her bottles until they shine. After delivering our three pints, Mr Watler walks briskly back down the path making a clicking noise through his teeth and Dolly moves two houses up the road. I run out excited to stroke her nose.

If Mr Watler doesn't click through his teeth he says, 'Gee up, Dolly,' or 'Gidde up.' But whatever he does, she responds.

'Such teamwork between man and beast,' Dad says. Horses are a common sight and welcome for other reasons. My father insists my mother shovel up the horse droppings, as good manure for the garden so even if she's in the middle of eating her breakfast she must run out, grab a shovel from the coal shed and scrape the horse dung off the road and then show my dad. She seems proud to have a pile of number twos outside the back door.

Dolly is a clever horse, avoiding potholes in the road. Roads like ours are full of rubble, broken bricks, rubbish and even glass with potholes as big as Mum's deep, white sink. Tarmacadam is available and tarmacked roads are the new novelty but only the council house roads have tarmac. Our house is near the bottom of the road. People walk by and stare into our living room. Mum buys net curtains.

'That'll sort them.'

'Why is our road so bumpy?'

'Well, lass. We'll have to pay for our road to be made up.'

I know we can't always have things if we have to pay for them. I don't use the word poor exactly but Mum is always saying we can't afford something or it's too expensive.

'Perhaps in a few years,' says Dad. He is patient. He never complains. As long as he has his twenty Senior Service and some seeds for his garden he is happy.

The garden is his pride and joy. Generally we don't need to buy vegetables as my father has green fingers and grows sufficient for the family. He doesn't grow potatoes as he says they're cheap in the shops. The whole back garden beyond the rockery at Grove Avenue is devoted to vegetable growing, with rows of cabbages, purple and white sprouts, runner beans, broad beans, rows of lettuces and also tomato plants, marrows and cucumbers. Dad has a cold frame where he grows early lettuces before the frosts finish. The sun keeps the cold frame warm. He had made it himself with offcuts of wood and an old window. One of my jobs in the summer is watering the tomatoes. Each plant having a flower pot inserted alongside. This method prevents the base of the plant rotting.

As people move into Grove Avenue, they take the rubble they clear and throw it into the ruts. The ashes from our grate are also used in the potholes and, on nice days, I take out bucket-loads of stones left by the builders. Now cyclists don't fall off when their front wheel hits a hole. This saves Dolly extra trips to the blacksmith. One Saturday, Mr Watler says I can go to watch the blacksmith put new shoes on Dolly, so I cycle with my mother and walk along the lower High Street to the forge – a fierce fire. He heats up metal until it's red – and then he can bend the iron into any shape, horseshoes or tools. Working horses need metal shoes to protect their hooves and the hot metal is put on the horse's hoof. I stifle a scream.

'It doesn't hurt,' says the blacksmith seeing my face. The hoof is a dead area, like your nails.

'She hasn't any nails,' says Mum. 'She bites them right down to the quick.'

* * *

Other things are better too. For the first two years I see more of my Weston grandparents and start going to Sunday school, while Mum attends St John's church. Everyone knows my mum and dad. People say hello everywhere we go. Also, now Mum is living in Southdown again, we begin to go to the St John's Young Wives' Group, organised by the vicar's wife. On fine days we sit on a blanket in the vicarage garden.

1950

'What's a detached house?' I've told a friend where I live.

'Where you walk all the way around the outside.'

'What, no neighbours through the walls?'

'Yes.'

But in our first months at Grove Avenue we can't actually walk all around the house. The outside of number 22 resembles a building site and the path at the side is blocked with sand, gravel and rubbish while my dad works on the garden. The day I arrive I only want to see Pam.

'Not to worry.' Dad sees my face. Of course he can sort anything out. Mum calls him Mr Fixit. I run round past the back door to see if Pam's safe. I'm feeling sick. When her hutch was loaded on the van, she peered through the wire netting looking frightened.

Now, I see the hutch placed precariously on the rubble but she bounces up and down inside, thumping her back legs and seems in good spirits.

'It'll soon look like the garden at Lea Valley.' I could run round our garden in Manor Road on concrete windy paths, avoiding plants Dad calls herbaceous borders. That garden burst with flowering shrubs so broken bricks, wood piles and paint tins are unexpected.

'We'll clear the ground.' He meant me when he said we. It's true. I love doing jobs.

Mum is bemused at the state of the garden. There's not even a path to the front door. When it rains that first autumn, the whole site sinks into a mud bath. Rainy days leave us with soaking lace-up shoes, squelching socks and cold wet feet. And the smell of builder's dust and paint. The air is full of pongs. Some good, of course, like the scent of new wood.

Mum isn't happy about mud and we spend the winter with newspaper on the floor inside the back door and lobby. Granny Weston gives us old carpet which we put down between the kitchen and dining area. Eventually Mum says she can't stand it anymore and Dad goes to Putterills and orders some ballast and gravel.

The house is not that warm. Mum lights a coal fire but it takes hours to make the room warm. When I am about five we get oil and paraffin heaters which stand on the landing and in the hall. I must not be clumsy near them. Yes, I am one of the clumsiest kids.

So no-one is happier than my mother when the warmer weather arrives in March and April. As good as his word, with lighter evenings, Dad turns the bare ground into something more hospitable. He spends evenings and weekends mixing up small quantities of cement, putting them into a rectangular wooden frame in the place where the slabs are needed. When it's set hard, usually by the next evening, he removes the wood to use for the next slab. He makes one slab a night in the summer evenings, when he can afford cement powder.

'I'll start with the path from the gate to the front door.' Dad's off out on a Sunday morning in his wellies.

One reason Dad can't always afford more cement is he is buying plants and fruit bushes. However, gradually he makes a path round the back garden. Between the slabs, Dad grows small quantities of grass seed. Later I have the job of clipping it back with the shears so the slab is free of mud and grass.

'Be careful not to tread on the wet cement.' Dad's warning as I run out of the house to feed Pam in the mornings. Once or twice I accidentally step on it but I wipe the cement off my shoes so Mum doesn't see.

Creative and artistic, my father designs the garden layout, so before the second spring, he digs the area he plans for a lawn in the back garden and plants seed. A broom handle, an old shirt and hat make a scarecrow. Another way to keep the birds away is to pierce holes in foil milk bottle tops and thread them on string.

They tinkle in the lightest breeze. Nothing upsets my dad except for neighbouring cats that come into our garden and scratch up the soil. At such times he's not averse to throwing the odd stone or lump of mud in their direction.

Within days small wisps of green appear. Dad's next job is a path across this soon-to-be lawn so Mum doesn't stand on wet soil or mud when hanging out washing. Nothing is too much trouble if it's for my mum. Behind he builds two rockeries and a wooden seat.

Halfway down the garden on the right-hand side, an oak tree stands on the boundary with number 20. Dad carves out a wooden swing from scrap wood and hangs it with strong rope from a thick bough.

I spend hours on this swing, day-dreaming, planning the next stage of my book or often just in a world of my own. I stand on one leg or try to hang upside down to imitate trapeze artists in Bertram Mills' circus. Soon, Dad puts paving slabs up to the oak tree. Some he puts round the swing so Mum can walk round it when she takes peelings and tea leaves to the compost heap. The only other time she goes down the path is to cut a cabbage for dinner.

'Can I take the rubbish out?' There's a good reason for my willingness, as this is the only time I'm allowed matches.

'I'll show you so you can do it yourself.' That's my dad. The next minute he has struck a match on the side of the box. Beyond the swing an old dustbin with its base broken open is used as an incinerator and here I burn paper and cardboard.

Everything we buy is put in paper bags. Tins are put in the dustbin, there being little other food packaging. Mum puts picnic sandwiches into greaseproof paper with an elastic band round them. Our dustbins are emptied weekly despite the few items inside but slowly plastic wrapping appears and increasingly finds its way into the dustbin.

Over time, I'm allowed to pick fruit, cut perpetual spinach – up to half the plant – stone the garden, weed between the lettuces and runner beans. I know which beans to pick and which bolted lettuces to give my rabbit and Daisy the tortoise.

The garden is my paradise.

September 1953

It's time for junior school! In September I start at Manland in Townsend Lane. I trudge in lace-up walking shoes, three miles there and three miles home in all weathers. I walk from Grove Avenue, to the Rose and Crown bus stop, take the bus to The George, then walk up Station Road under the railway bridge and left into Carlton Road. Sometimes I get off at the Cock Public House and walk up Sun Lane. Eventually, Dad reckons I'm safe to ride my bike with him and leave it in the room behind the shop.

I pass the red brick building where I was born – the Red House – and then right into a private road, Thomson's Close, which leads to Stewart Road and then Manland Avenue. Sir Halley Stewart, a local philanthropist, bought the Red House in 1904 and in 1929 he gifted it to the people of Harpenden for a hospital. A fete in 1930 raised money for the refurbishment. Stewart Road, named after him, is a rough track.

Christmas will soon be here. I've asked for the book *Black Beauty* and a doll with hair that can be washed. As soggy autumn arrives, we can't play on the field but crowd into the playground playing hopscotch and skipping.

At the first sign of frost I can't wait to get there. Snow is even better. The bigger boys slide down the steep tarmac making slides. We queue to run and slide. It's better not to fall out with big boys or you could be banned.

In January we wake to a large snowfall. However, school is never closed. Most teachers live within walking or cycling distance. Few can afford cars. Whatever the weather I am sent clad in warm clothing with two pairs of socks inside my wellington boots. Complaining isn't an option. When there's severe ice, I'm unable to ride my bicycle and buses don't come, I have to walk past the frozen ponds at the foot of the Common. These virtual ice rinks are a magnet for local children but it's more than my life is worth to go on the ice.

'A boy fell through the ice once,' my mum says, 'and he nearly died!'

Twenty minutes of sliding and no-one can stand up straight. At the end of playtime, when the whistle blows, I line up with my classmates, then shuffle my feet until I am within an arm's reach of the next pupil, put a hand on their shoulder, shuffle again to make a space the length of my arm and when the whistle blows again I turn with everyone else to form a straight line. On the last whistle we march into school, left right, left right just like the army blokes my dad talks about. Perfect timing or you'll be for it.

Once back in class, it takes forever for the next playtime. What if the snow doesn't last? We sneak glances through the window, look up at the sky when teacher's busy with another pupil. We can't concentrate on sums and spelling although to be caught looking out of the window heralds a reprimand, being kept in at playtime or, at worst, a rap on the knuckles with a ruler.

At last the bell and it's time for our bottle of milk. Teachers stand over us to make sure we drink every last drop. Then we race through the corridors grabbing coats from hooks outside the classroom, past the rancid smell of the boys' toilets and out into the dazzling sunlight. Queues on the playground slides are orderly and teachers on playground duty warn of sun on snow and wet ice. Running in front of an ice-jetting pupil is a hazard but we don't care. Snowball fights, common and not forbidden, leave us dripping in white wet mush although putting stones inside a snowball is a punishable offence.

Regardless of the weather, boys have fights and a crowd gathers around the two enemies all shouting for their favoured protagonist, a buzz of 'Fight! Fight!' rises to fever pitch. A male teacher intervenes and asks the two fighters to shake hands and make up. No boy is ever chastised or sent to the headmaster for fighting. Amazingly, despite this, there's less violence both inside and outside schools in the 1950s.

As autumn approaches, we play conkers although I prefer to collect them and polish them until they shine and reflect my face. Other crazes are cat's cradle – wool wound around the hands while another child takes the strands in a certain way and the pattern then increases in complexity.

I trot off to school with my skipping rope, swirling it over my head all the way to the bus and at playtime two girls hold the rope while others run in to skip. There are rhymes we chant while skipping. There are games of Jacks and five stones, yoyo competitions and more. A piece of stray chalk in the classroom is secreted in a pocket, kept until playtime and used to draw a hop-scotch, another queue I happily join. Then we find a spare wall on the school building and play with a ball on elastic hitting it above and below your other hand.

In class there are new demands, though my enthusiasm for creativity and fictional pursuits never wavers. Now juniors, we are required to write in ink! Our double desks hold our exercise books and have lift-up lids. At the top right-hand side of the desk is a hole for the inkpot. The ink monitor is required to replenish the inkwells every morning. Our writing implement is a wooden stick with a metal nib pushed on the end. The art of neat writing is to dip your pen in the inkwell just enough to make the nib inky but not so full that it drips.

The trick is to blot it at the end of each line so that our hands don't smear the ink from the line above. I am frequently making blobs on my exercise book which require dabbing with blotting paper. I am a messy writer. I envy those with clean exercise books as mine never stand up to scrutiny.

The post-war baby boom ensures tightly packed classrooms – fifty children per class, all offspring of returning servicemen in 1945. I am eight years old when I move up to Manland but some children are still only seven. The double desks are in five lines and each line is five deep. The row nearest to the teacher's desk (and the window!) is the line for brighter, more academically able children and some teachers even label the rows A to E which aids identification but reinforces the streaming rampant in the fifties.

Boys frequently play about with the ink despite the risk of the slipper or a whack from the ruler. The proximity of the desks is temptation itself to the boys as, despite teachers' remonstrations, they often dip the long pigtail or the ties of girls' summer dresses into their inkwells. The desks are so close, it's easy to do. Many a girl faces the dismay on her mother's face and a sharp rebuke if she comes out of school with an inky pigtail or strap.

One morning, the boys behind me tie the straps from my summer dress to my chair, so at playtime I am unable to move and am left struggling to undo their tightly-knotted efforts. My first teacher, Miss F, is a strict disciplinarian. No-one messes in her class. Her forte is a whack the back of the legs. Thank goodness I'm a good learner – some slower children can't learn to read, spell or learn their tables. I pray every day I will get to July without the dreaded slap on the legs. Most days, several times the sound of the smack on the legs flies through the air – rebounding with such force, the recipient jumps with pain. Some boys are slapped every day. My school photo shows a white-faced, tight-lipped child, noticeably strained. No-one complained about teachers and slaps, ruler whacks, the slipper and cane were commonplace.

'It'll be worth it,' my aunt insists. 'Miss F has a reputation for getting children through the eleven-plus.'

Each Monday Miss F hands out slips of paper with ten or twenty spellings on them. She has handwritten fifty slips individually. It must have taken her all weekend. These spellings must be learnt so we're word perfect. My parents sit each Monday night and take it in turns to help me learn the spellings. My mother dreads the Monday slip of paper and the agony of an evening on the task. And so do I. Mum and I repeat them over and over – saying the letters out loud, the only way I know to learn.

After labouring Monday evening, I wake and repeat the spellings as I walk to school for the horror of the Tuesday Test. Pupils get a slap for every incorrect spelling. I tremble until I realise if I can learn the spellings I can stay slap-free. I become a good speller by sheer determination to avoid marks on my legs.

Many of my classmates are preceded by older brothers and sisters but I have no such link that curries favour with teachers. It must be good to have an older sibling who helps with spellings and arithmetic such as long division. Although at other times … I watch a boy faltering on the eight times table, rapped with a ruler.

'Your brother would've known that by heart!'

He's used as an example to the rest of us. At such times, I'm pleased I have a sister tucked away in a special school in Sussex. Luckily, I thrive on academic work. I ask for extra homework.

Craft activities, however, leave me wanting. On Monday and Wednesday afternoons, we have knitting class. One Wednesday I drop a stitch and, when I try to pick it up, the lower rows dissolve before my eyes, leaving a small hole. The more I poke with the needle, the bigger and blacker the hole becomes until it descends into a major chasm. I hide it in my hands too scared to show it.

The girl at the next desk sees what's happened.

'You'll cop it for that!' But I am determined to avoid the infamous slap.

The next Monday I develop a cracking good dose of bronchitis, such that I'm allowed to stay off school. I sneak some flour from the cupboard to put on my face. My heart sinks when Mum says I might have to go to the doctor.

Dr Akeroyd's surgery is in Rothamsted Avenue. He gives us a prescription which we take to Spackman's chemist. The chemist's daughter, Hazel, is sort of related as she married Auntie Alice's son, Bob Woodward. If I have a fever, Mum calls the doctor out for a home visit. The doctors never complain.

I have no fever today. I haven't worked that one out yet.

On Tuesday my voice is a squeak.

'I feel a bit better.'

Then, by Tuesday evening I feign more illness so I have to stay home on Wednesday. I manage the same trick the following week, varying the symptoms slightly and contrive a different sickness on the Wednesday as suspicions are aroused.

The following Sunday finds me blowing my nose uncontrollably so once again I am allowed to stay at home but my mother insists I return on the Wednesday. I hear my dad and mum talking.

'Making it up,' says Dad.

Eventually Mum prises the problem out of me and tells me I must take my knitting bag to the teacher. I am horrified when, that afternoon, I am called first. As I near the desk I shake at the sight of the severe lined face and grey hair curled up tightly with pins. My knees wobble, my legs twitch and my tummy is hard.

If only, I think, the floor would open up and swallow me whole, like Jonah in the whale. The woollen mess of knots and tangles looks worse than ever.

'What's happened here?' Her tone is clipped and sharp. She frowns at the tangled mess. Any minute now I will feel it.

But no. I can't believe my luck. She sorts it out in minutes, unravelling the knitting until the wool unrolls beyond the hole and lifting the stitches on to the needle. I make my way back to my seat with great relief!

Later I wonder if my mother phoned the school. Or, perhaps I was let off because I am good at spelling and maths. Perhaps she likes me and empathises with an academic child who struggles with practical subjects. If so, working hard in arithmetic and English is a lesson not lost on me.

But I don't always escape reprimands. One day my mother meets me after school. I am quite excited. During the final afternoon lesson I ask to go to the toilet so I can see whether she's outside the door. Another child left the room earlier so I have no reason to think this is unacceptable. Mum looks askance.

'Is it all right to come out?'

'Oh, yes.' I say gaily. 'We all do it.'

Five minutes later the bell goes. A roar from Miss Franklin sends my heart racing and I jump near out my skin.

'Dinah, you will stay in and make up the time you lost going out to the toilet.' My heart sinks and, on the verge of tears, I watch the others file out to collect their coats. I'm embarrassed, my cheeks burn – I'm sure they're red. I hope no-one sees the tears in my eyes. Worse, I am in for a second telling off for being kept in. Mum reckons I am naughty anyway. But for now, she waits patiently outside until I am dismissed.

'Right, you can go,' says Miss F, her face still broadcasting the usual fierce expression. It's too late though. We are late. My mother is silent all the way.

* * *

After Miss F's class we move up to Miss Hairy Legs. She's strict but not as fearsome as Miss F.

Now I find myself struggling with long division and wishing my sister was home. Luckily, a friend who lives in the same road comes to the rescue.

I hear Mum talking about them.

Her father was a distinguished scientist who refused to work for the Nazis in the war. They fled Czechoslovakia and now he works at the Rothamsted Experimental Station.

Mum knocked on their door and asked if their daughter could help me.

'They were the lucky ones,' she said.

And so was I when she showed me long division.

* * *

'What sort of shoe do you want?' The assistant in Blindells measures my feet but my mother ignores her question. I daren't answer especially as I would love a pair of those little shoes with one strap across that I see in the shop window.

Brown lace-ups. Mum never veers away from the ugly and heavy when buying my shoes. I blame my father with his love of leather and his belief that ill-fitting shoes are bad for children's feet.

No, not those, too fashionable. The assistant is waved away and sent to the back storeroom to provide an alternative.

'Start-Rites. They'll do.' I inwardly sigh.

Then the girl takes me to a machine and I am invited to look through the window and see if my toes are far enough away from the front of the shoe.

'Room to grow, is there?' Mum can't keep quiet. She thinks she knows more than the assistant.

As we leave the shop, she continues.

No scraping the toes when you are on the swing. No going in puddles or kicking footballs with the boys. One day, I think ...

The rest of my attire also leaves much to be desired. Girls are obliged to wear a gym slip and I have long hand-knitted socks. Later, some children have shop-bought socks, which I envy. Another embarrassment is wearing regulation navy blue knickers for indoor gym and dancing with only our school blouse and knickers. Mum insists I wear a pair of white knickers underneath the navy ones. I didn't need to disclose this undressing for indoor PE or outdoor netball. However, in summer we go to Kimpton Swimming Pool and, oh dear, girls have to share changing rooms. I try to undress discreetly. When detected I say navy blue knickers make me itch and pray she won't divulge my secret.

December 1953

'We're skint.' I hear the word long before I know what it means.

Mum is rolling pastry, her red puffy hands chafed from scrubbing Dad's shirt collars. How can green Bibby soap make things white? She uses her apron as a towel to rub the flour off and sinks into the fireside chair for a well-earned rest. It's my sign for a cuddle as I spread across her lap, feel her strong hands hold me firm, but back in the summer the hugging was short lived.

'There's a surprise for you down the garden.'

Another rabbit? I think. Company for Pam?

I scramble down and run out of the back door without stopping to close it.

'Born in a barn were you?' Mum's voice chases me in the wind.

I gather speed, my Clark's sandals barely touching the ground, as I veer round the side of the corrugated iron shed to the concrete path. I avoid treading on the grass between the slabs in case a lion jumps out of the hedge. Mum and Dad don't know about the lions.

Pam's hutch sits on stilts under the privet hedge between us and those noisy people over the back. It's a speck in the distance near Dad's cold frame where his seeds are poking through into the warmth. I duck to avoid the low branch of our pear tree where the snakes hide. They kill with one flick of the tongue.

Pam wrinkles her nose, twitching and thumping her back legs. Excitement or hunger? I am not sure. I pull some leaves off Dad's spring cabbage. I am allowed. Even the brownish and yellow leaves are nibbled at speed.

There's no new rabbit. No second pet. Unsurprising really as Mum is always reproaching me for my neglect.

Last week it was, 'Clean out the hutch! It stinks.'

And I vow to but as usual I forget. There's so much to do avoiding lions and snakes and writing my stories.

Later I find Dad has done it inducing Mum's wrath.

'It's her responsibility,' she growls, glaring, daring me to look complacent. But Dad is whistling and sending me a sneaky wink.

Today, Saturday, Dad won't be home on time. It's his monthly short back and sides at the barber's in Station Road. When he comes in with his trousers tucked down with cycle clips and his bicycle put in the shed, Mum will tell him he looks good. But for now there is just me and the surprise down the garden.

All I see is Pam leaping about in her hutch. On her own.

So no second rabbit but then I see the surprise. To the right of the rabbit hutch is a wire-netted area I thought was put there ready for more plants. Dad is always building something for his gardening. It's made of wood. He prepared it at the weekend and inside – a new addition since last night – a little wooden house. But I am not seeing the house.

On the mud and pecking at seed are two balls of yellow fluff.

I jump at a step behind me.

'Chicks?'

'Yes. You might like the job of feeding them.'

'Yes, yes, yes.'

Mum laughs seeing me so excited.

As she returns to the house, I am still bouncing, my hair bunches thumping on the back of my neck, my school uniform dress flapping at my knees.

'I will, I will.'

She stops, turns and I see her expression is cloudy.

'Just don't get too attached to them!'

With that she stoops down to cut a cabbage. My heart sinks. Greens! Another painful dinner full of gagging on savoys, scoldings, the odd slap and forbidden pudding.

My eyes follow her. Why does she always spoil everything? Why give me fluffy chicks to feed and then go cut a cabbage, yuk? I hope the lions get her.

Ignoring her last words, I name the chicks Peter and Paul and fall hopelessly in love. In the weeks that follow I leap out of bed without being called ten times, wash, dress and take food to them, whatever the weather, braving the lions in the hedge, clutching the paper bag of chicken feed to my chest. I talk to them. Heck, I am such a lonely kid with my deaf sister at boarding school! The birds cheep, their beady eyes glinting and every cluck answering my chatter. They appear to grow before my eyes, their clucking getting stronger and louder by the day.

I dread mealtimes. Most of Mum's dinners are what she calls cheap cuts in the butcher's. I am given a few florins and a ten shilling note and sent shopping with a list. Our butcher, Mr Conrath, knows us so I think he understands about the skint thing. He hacks away at red carcasses, chucks pieces on the scales, wraps them before calling out the price.

'Pay the missus,' he says. Mrs C sits in a booth.

'Hello, Dinah,' she says taking the money. Out on the street, I call in at Boniface's and buy spangles and refreshers. I stuff several in my mouth at a time. If you suck really slowly, you can make a spangle last twenty minutes. I get change from my thrupenny bit.

Meanwhile, on other days, Mum continues to dish up questionable items on my plate. Pigs' trotters I wish had kept trotting, streaky pork that oozes grease enough to make me retch and – worse – bacon dumplings. And alongside … the hated spinach or purple sprouting and boiled potatoes. On really bad days the awful orange stuff called swede. Mum is not the world's best cook and the least adventurous. That new Italian food smells, she says. Good old English, you can't beat it. She dollops lumpy mash, stringy cabbage and meat in an untidy pile with about as much decorum as when she adds scraps to the compost heap. Presentation isn't her thing.

It's not all bad though. Harpenden Villagers, in years gone by, reckoned they could get the children back at teatime merely by shouting, 'Swimmers!!' outside the front door. Made from flour and suet, similar to dumplings, they were rolled flat like pastry and cooked in a pan of shallow boiling water. We devour them with jam or golden syrup and never leave a scrap.

'Eat your greens,' Granny says. 'And you'll grow big and strong.' Who wants to? Even at eight years of age I fancy myself as one of the kidnapped girls in *Seven Brides for Seven Brothers*. They're all slim and pretty and obviously didn't eat theirs.

Greens. Yuk. I try the 'I feel sick' excuse without luck.

Then, Granny's favourite line, 'The starving people in Africa would be pleased to eat that,' also falls on deaf ears.

'Parcel it up then,' I mutter, 'and send it.'

Far worse, Granny chimes dire warnings that Father Christmas won't come as I shuffle unwanted, foul tasting and unrecognisable items around my plate.

Once down away from the table I forget but, on Christmas Eve, a niggling thought returns that my flippancy come Christmas morning might lead to an empty sock. Too late perhaps, I regret the cabbage I hid under my potato, and the Brussel sprouts I sneaked into my pinny pocket for Pam. Also, I am not averse to sneaking spinach or lumpy swede into my lap and then to the floor where I mash it flat under my foot as I slither down from the table. So what! It's a dark green carpet with beige flecks. But my discards, hiding within the tufts, often jam up the Ewbank.

Summer meanders by and the October frost hardens the leaves which begin to crunch beneath my feet as I dodge the lions on the path. Peter and Paul have fattened up Mum says and I yearn to pick them up, cuddle them, talk to them, tell them my secrets and warn them about the lions. I want to say I will care for them and no-one will hurt them. They are my only friends.

Schooldays rattle by heading for the Christmas holidays. School dinners are tasteless, cardboard meat with white soggy mashed potato and peas like bullets. Sour-faced dinner ladies stand over us and force us to eat our plates clean. Never mind if we gag. The minced meat pie and shepherd's pie are OK and the jam sponge isn't bad if the lumpy custard misses it. As the days get colder, Mum gets out her steaming cloths and I dream of treacle pudding only to find steak and kidney on my plate. The meat is grisly and the kidney chewy.

I still wake early, to the sound of clucking ringing in my ears, tumble out of bed and scuttle down the now brown and dying garden in my gabardine mackintosh. Peter and Paul flap their feathers. They're big now, Peter being the fattest. Their beaks are fearsome, jabbing at the wire and pecking my legs. I am disappointed, I'd hoped they'd be more tame but, at this spot, my world is peaceful and my tummy isn't tight. The lions and snakes don't frighten me anymore. In fact, I haven't thought about them for weeks. And, just for once I am glad I live here with Mum and Dad. Dougie down the road hasn't got chicken pets and Linda up the road hasn't even got a rabbit.

Suddenly I have friends who want to call round, knock on the door and trot down the garden path to see my chickies. They're jealous. Fancy that!

Then, before I know it we have our church carol concert and finish school for the holidays. Mum is busy with the Christmas cake, puddings and grocery orders. I love this time of year. When not in the kitchen, she's wrapping presents behind her bedroom door and shouting, 'Don't come in!' I love it all. The whole shebang! It makes my heart beat fast and my voice sings loud and clear the Christmas songs I hear on the *Light Programme.*

Carol singers croon outside the front door – another exception to the back door rule – and, when I answer, I am allowed a few pennies for their tin. If they are from the church, Mum gives a shilling. Her large form looms behind me and if the singing dies down, she says, 'Sing another verse or you won't get any money!'

Only three days to Christmas, I am getting excited, the tree's in a bucket in the hall and the path is frosty when I scoot down it to see Peter and Paul. On my way back I pass Mrs Jenkins from number 18 and my dad. They are talking about weight and money. Dad tells me to start decorating the Christmas tree so we can light the candles.

The clocks are on a go slow. I can't wait for Christmas Day. I dream of my much coveted present. A naked doll with hair I can brush and wash. Granny's knitted dolls' clothes in another parcel. Soon my sister and I will wake to goodies on the bottom of our beds. Then it'll be off to church with Mum when we have to act religious, singing all the bits and pieces along with the rest of the congregation.

My sister is five years older but she keeps the fairy tale of Father Christmas alive for me playing along with the adults with the story that the man with the white beard came down the chimney despite it being made up with coal slack and chimbles and set to burn throughout the night.

We're keen to hang up our Christmas stocking – not that it is a stocking. We hang up knee-length socks in great excitement and then, on Christmas Eve, we always find it difficult to sleep. Once awake, we start to feel the outside of the socks which are lumpy and use a torch to speak to each other wondering what is inside. There are a few nuts, a satsuma or tangerine, some sweets, a pencil and perhaps a yoyo or magic slate. The presents from one of our aunties are always in our stocking, swelling the booty and making interesting lumps in the socks which we prod in the darkness before it's time to get up.

First, Christmas Eve and another duty visit to the chicken pen but today there's no clucking. My heart misses a beat. My stomach shifts downward. Flapping in the wind is the door to the pen. They've gone. Peter and Paul have vanished. My heart lurches with fear. My legs shake and my mouth drops open. I run back to the house screaming to find my sister grinning and Mum and Dad arguing about whose fault it is that I am so upset. Then the terrible realisation that the lump of meat and bone that Mum has in her hands is actually one of my pets.

The Big Day and the doll under the tree can't bring the joy I expected. My heart is heavy and I have hardly slept. It has to be the worst Christmas Day ever. At the dinner table we pull crackers, plonk paper hats on our heads and the others sing 'we wish you a merry Christmas'. My voice won't come but the tears do. Granny has arrived and we must be good and happy as it's hard for her at Christmas without Granddad. No-one mentions Peter and Paul. I loved my granddad, but my fluffy chicks, now grown into clucking hens, were my family. Nobody understands. The whole family laughs, making jokes about wringing necks, plucking feathers and stuffing which doesn't mean much then although as I think about it ...

I sit glum and straight-faced staring at my plate. Fresh in my memory are all those happy mornings, the cackling and clucking, twinkling beady eyes, scratching claws, the conversations, the way the lions and snakes seem to have disappeared and here in front of me is something called chicken. Before dinner Mum sat me down and gave me one of her lessons where she tries to get me to understand things. 'It was only a bird. Humans have to eat meat and everyone in England is eating chicken on Christmas Day. You see, we don't have much money. In fact, we're skint most of the time but this year one of your uncles gave us those two chicks. Mrs Jenkins paid Dad for one the other day. How do you think we could afford that doll? We're not made of money. We're lucky we have enough to eat. Now come out of your room, go downstairs and get to the table.'

'Eat it all up like a good girl.'

I am still sitting staring, my stomach in a hard knot, a sick feeling creeping up my throat. I think I might even ...

My sister is laughing. I can't bear it. I hate them all. Tears roll down my cheeks, leaving salty dribble on my lips. How can I eat Peter who listened to all my sorrows, worries over learning my tables and heard me recite my spellings every Tuesday? Silence falls over the table, the hats don't shine so brightly now and no-one is looking at me. Everyone is staring downwards. Nobody speaks. My family are all digging forks into Peter and putting him in their mouths. I can almost hear him cheeping inside their throats.

Out of the corner of my eye I see Mum raise her eyebrows at my father and get up. She comes round to my side of the table and picks up my plate.

'Never mind,' she says, 'I have something else for you.'

I watch her take the plate and shovel the contents into the bin.

'Would you like some Christmas meat instead of chicken?'

I nod. I am hungry after all. Then she disappears into the larder. In seconds she's back with a new plate of food.

'What is it?' My sister thinks she's missing something.

'It's Christmas meat,' says my mother.

Then, putting it in front of me, 'There, it's much nicer than roast chicken.'

Dad lifts up my cracker which I've ignored so far.

'Blow your whistle,' he laughs, picking up a piece of red plastic and blowing it.

'I love Christmas,' says Granny, wiping a tear, murmuring about missing her Bert and soon the room is jolly.

Mum was right. Christmas meat is much nicer than roast chicken and five minutes later my plate is empty.

Monday Wash – A Mangle, A Clothes Horse and A Boiler

Regardless of the weather, washing day is always Monday. From our upstairs windows across the back hedges, rows of washing lines flap in the wind. Newly-starched whites blow like flags. Few lines are full on other days and no-one dares hang washing out on Sundays. But, the few working mothers must do theirs on Saturdays. Most classmates go to church whether Methodist, Presbyterian or Church of England. Only nurses and doctors work on Sundays, shops are closed and pubs open at lunch time.

The washing machine is as yet unknown, so my mother hand-washes sheets and shirts, even blankets, then rinses them, using a wringer we call a mangle which is ostracised in the outhouse behind the garage, because the kitchenette is so tiny. Two rollers squeeze out the water and the starch. Mum lets me turn the handle. She passes the washing between the rollers. The items come out dry. Mum folds items steeped in starch before mangling. This removes creases and makes ironing easier. Washing starts at 8am. Mum scrubs clothes on her wooden draining board, using either Fairy soap or Bibby's green. A blue bag in the boiler makes the whites brighter.

On cold days I love sitting by the coal fire. The heat turns my legs red. When Mum takes a break from her chores, she lets me sit on her lap. Her white hands are puckered and soggy from a morning in hot water, her knuckles blood red and grazed from scrubbing. The red fades leaving red blotchy skin despite liberal doses of Vaseline hand cream. As she strokes my hair the scent of Fairy soap tickles my nose and her hand tastes of hand cream. Her legs gleam red and scaly through her stockings, from crouching over the coal fire.

Mum sings all morning with windows opened wide to allow steam to escape. I love school holidays or if I am off school sick, as, while the soprano gives her all, I can watch flames lick up the chimney, coal crackling as it burns. Everywhere feels cosy and at peace.

'Move yourself.' Mum brings wet washing to hang on the wooden rack at the fireplace. She calls this her clothes horse but it doesn't look like a horse. She stokes up the fire, the red glow making steam rise from the wet clothes. I use the clothes horse to play house and play schools and libraries with my dollies and teddies. I give spelling tests – one teddy is a really bad speller! I make library tickets and put ticketholders inside the front covers of the books. I stick paper on the next page using a date stamp to stamp books out for a week. My teddies must pay fines for overdue books. I have toy money for that.

Our cord washing line stretches the full width of our back lawn. Dad's new paving stones save Mum's shoes from the mud. The cord has a thick coating of black chimney soot so Mum wipes it first.

She holds up the cloth and says, 'Look at this!'

On Tuesday ironed clothes are returned to the clothes horse to air and then taken upstairs to the airing cupboard. Mum is fussy about airing clothes. We mustn't wear anything damp. Sometimes I help with the ironing. To save electricity, Mum folds everything before switching on the iron. She folds hankies once and pillowcases twice. She folds sheets into eight and then changes the surface by turning and refolding them.

Eventually my parents have more money and Mum has a laundry man collect the sheets and towels. She includes Granny Weston's laundry.

'This makes it worth it,' she says. It saves drying towels and sheets now my sister is at home and we are both growing.

January 1954

I wake up aware of a chill breeze on my cheeks. I throw myself at the curtains to pull them but they're stuck fast to the frost inside the window. On the ground is what I'm praying for. I press my hands together and say, 'Thank you, God.' At last! Everywhere is white.

Snow! Now I can use the sledge Dad made. We live on a hill so we can claim full rights to the road in snowy weather. Only one or two council house people own cars and they've walked past in wellington boots, their cars abandoned in the Big Freeze.

I grab my clothes and rush downstairs, the stairs and hall so cold my breath makes steam in front of my face, like Dad smoking his Senior Service. Mum is preparing breakfast.

'Up early I see.' A smile peeps out the corner of her mouth. She's in a good mood so I'll make the most of it. Perhaps she likes snow too.

Dad has lit the fire so I hover nearby and put my clothes on the fireguard. This is dangerous I know but there are two adults in the room and they do it for me if I don't. I wait for the clothes to warm up and then pull off my pyjamas and dive into vest and jumpers.

The kitchen diner has windows both ends. It's known as double aspect. From the kitchen end, we look down the garden, now white with bare twigs poking out to show where the grass finishes and the garden begins. From the front we see people slipping and sliding. Both living rooms have open fireplaces. The kitchen fireplace has a damper at the back of the grate. This is pushed in or pulled out to direct warmth to heat the water or to heat the room.

'Push the damper in,' Mum says, 'so you feel the warmth.' And I do so with the little poker.

Amazingly, I'm allowed to carry out tasks with the fire. My parents are safety conscious but open fires are the only form of heating. The rest of the house is icy cold.

'I have seen an electric fire in Kingston House,' Mum says.

'I'll go and take a look,' says Dad.

'Do you think it's safe?' Mum's face is tight.

I don't want to move away from the fire but Mum insists I sit at the table for breakfast. Today she has fried bacon. Once away from the fire, I shiver and can't wait to get back to the fireside chair.

'Dinah, your legs are younger than mine ...' I dread these words as it means I'm to be asked to run an errand and, in cold weather, it will be to fetch something from upstairs, now more like the polar arctic circle which we've learnt about at school. Mum's bag is upstairs and I am to get it.

'Don't forget your hot water bottle,' says Mum, 'you'll want it tonight.'

I shove my hands down the bed and find the cold

rubber. I take it downstairs and empty it down the sink. It hangs with three other hot water bottles in the pantry. We all take hot water bottles to bed. I know how to fill mine safely and press on the top half to expel the steam so it doesn't burst.

My feet itch when they touch the heat of the bottle at night.

'Chilblains,' Mum says using magic cream. They itch in the evening too when I am sitting by the fire.

But, for now, I want to enjoy the snow. I get my sledge from the shed. I have two pairs of socks inside my wellington boots, two sizes too big. I'm wearing a funny hat my granny knitted, Mum's scarf and gloves.

The insides of my knees are red and chapped. Every night Mum puts Vaseline on them. I flinch but daren't make a fuss. My sister doesn't get chapped knees or chilblains. She only has to go downstairs at boarding school to lessons. I envy her. No wet freezing walk to school for her. No big boys waiting in Thomson's Close to bully her to go apple scrumping.

Today is Saturday. A fire has already been lit. On school days the fire is laid ready for the afternoon when Mum gets home from the shop.

'It's a waste of money lighting a fire when everyone's out,' she says.

Before I come home from school, Mum lights a fire in the sitting room. This is so I am warm for my piano practice. When I go in I move the settee as, otherwise, I can't feel the warmth.

My mother has a gas cooker and, on cold mornings,

Dad lights a couple of rings to warm the kitchen area up. And there is always coal!

'Morning, Mrs Munt.' A sooty face appears at the back door. In the road another horse stands but, this time, hooked up to the coal cart. Like Dolly our milkman's horse, this horse has blinkers with studs so she'll not get scared of cars, scooters or bicycles.

The coalman, from Lockhart's in Station Approach, is smiling, the whites of his eyes glinting brightly in stark contrast to his black dusty face. He has his helper with him. They hump the Hessian sacks each holding one hundredweight of coal and pass the kitchen window stooping such that only their woolly hats show. Our coal shed is at the back of the house, behind a green door in the wall. The coalmen don't stand up straight until they have offloaded their cargo.

Every morning, my mother takes out the ashes from the previous day's fire and tips them next to the compost heap or on the garden according to my father's instructions. If there's snow or ice – a frequent occurrence – she sprinkles them on the path or in the road so their lingering warmth melts the snow.

Mum lays the fire each day with paper, wood and small pieces of coal she calls chimbles. I'm taught to do this before I am five. Once it has started burning, making up of the fire involves putting on more coal and adding shovels full of slack – small chippings of coal and coal dust from the bottom of the coal shed. My mother wets this slack to make it last longer at the back of the fire, although it makes the chimney belch black smoke. Sometimes she puts wet potato peelings on the back. Amazingly, the fire made up of wet slack and peelings sends out more heat than coal alone. I love sweeping the fireplace, with the little brush from the brass companion set that stands on the left in the fireplace, using the brass poker to make the ash drop through the grate, sweeping until all the coal dust has gone. Once the fire pulls through and glows red, we toast bread and crumpets, using a toasting fork.

Once a year we have the chimney sweep. Before Mr Vokins' visit, the carpet must be lifted and Mum covers the furniture to protect it from the soot. The sweep arrives on his bicycle with a large basket or pannier holding brushes and handles. He brings his brushes into the house, puts down one large cloth and fixes another cloth over the fireplace. Under this he pushes the brushes up the chimney. My mother books the sweep in the holidays. She knows we both love the experience.

Soon after the brushes are pushed up the chimney, the sweep sends us into the garden to look at the chimney and tell him when we see the brushes poke out of the top. We think this is fun but there is a reason. Soot damages lungs so it's safer for children to be outside. When the sweep has finished, he rolls up his cloths and takes them down the garden where he dumps the soot in a neat pile.

Soot causes problems elsewhere too. Mum travels to London in all weathers to take my sister back and forth to school. Sometimes I go with her but, if there's a thick fog – a pea-souper – I stay home. The five-day London smog in December 1952 was caused by industrial pollution and high pressure weather conditions and resulted in 4000 deaths.

Another horse and cart in Grove Avenue is the Rag and Bone Man. The man calls 'rag-bone' in a sing-song fashion sounding more like 'rah boo'. Rags convert into fabric or paper and bones make glue. He pays money for scrap iron.

Our porch has a light and Mum switches it on at dusk during the winter. It's a welcoming sight as my tired legs trudge up the road after a long day at school. At Christmas, there's added sparkle of our decorated Christmas tree. In the first years my parents use lighted candles on clips. Soon this is deemed dangerous and, by then, there are simple coloured fairy lights in the shops.

In the kitchen, a walk-in larder keeps food cool but, soon, Mum has her first electric fridge so the larder becomes our crockery cupboard which stores cooking ingredients and, as they gradually appear on the market, some tins. My parents have a fireside chair each and, in winter, sit either side of the fire reading the newspapers and talking. Mum is always knitting, socks for us, pullovers for Dad. I wear a ring of elastic or a garter at the top to hold up the socks.

One day, Dad puts up two shelves for Mum alongside this fireside chair for her sewing box, writing paper and pens. She enjoys doing crosswords and reading *Woman's Own*. A small pile of mending is usually awaiting attention.

On Wednesdays and Sundays my grandmother sits in Dad's chair and reads the papers talking to my mum at the same time.

At weekends I'm busy with my pets – Daisy the tortoise and Pam my rabbit. Next door at number 20 live Mr and Mrs Good. Their daughter, Betty, has a large aviary. One day she brings a baby bird with a broken wing for me to have as a pet.

'He can't go in the aviary or the other birds will pick on him,' she says.

I call him Peter. I love all animals. I'm a junior member of the PDSA – the Busy Bees – so I'm quick to say yes. He chatters to himself in the mirror and sits with the bell on his head. If he begins squawking we cover the cage to fool him that it's bedtime. Sometimes I arrive home from school to find the cage covered as his noise has driven Mum mad. When Peter dies, Betty brings round Bobby as a replacement. Every Saturday I go to the Village to buy cuttlefish, millet and bird seed from Woolworth's or a pet shop.

I am never without pets. Soon after my rabbit dies, I see a notice outside a house on Grove Road advertising baby bunnies for sale. I knock on the door – unbelievable I know – but everywhere was safe then or so we thought. A man takes me round the back of the house to two large hutches. He opens one door to reveal a heaving mass of wriggling black and white fur. Holding them up one at a time he asks which one I want. I have to wait a few weeks until my bunny can leave her mother. The happy day dawns when I go to the house, clutching some saved pocket money and a cardboard box to collect my new baby rabbit.

I name her Scruffy and carry her home the box clutched tightly to my chest.

Granddad's Signal Box

'Can I pull a signal?' I'm at the top of the wooden stairs to the signal box.

Granddad Munt works as a signalman at Harpenden East Station. This visit is a highlight of our school holiday. We cycled to Batford and visited our grandmother in Batford Road before walking via Batford Meadow where a path leads from the bottom of Batford Road to a footbridge over the River Lea. This is the path Granddad uses to walk to work.

I know what he's going to say.

'You can pull number nineteen.'

Then, 'It's your birthday number.'

Of course it's a dead signal but I don't know that.

However, there are more delights pulling the fully-operational signal as a train is due.

We've left our bikes on the path that leads back to Station Road.

'No need to padlock them.' Mum's striding ahead.

In school holidays we pay at least one visit to our Batford grandparents, cycling with Mum from Grove Avenue via The Greenway and then turning right into High Firs

Crescent. When we reach the Wheathampstead Road we take the narrow, winding country road, Sewer Lane, leading to the Lower Luton Road. Sometimes we cycle via Crabtree Lane to the ford where children go fishing. Then we turn into Coldharbour Lane where my great-grandfather, Arthur Tuffin, lived in the 1800s. Their house is no longer there.

'Get off and walk round.' We are at the ford but we ignore Mum and prefer to pedal through at high speed and make a big splash. If it has been raining heavily Mum worries it's too deep.

Once at 30 Batford Road, Grandma Munt and my great-grandmother, Small Grandma – so called because of her diminutive size – sit waiting in the kitchen, but I don't want to go in. The lure of the old cast iron pump in the back garden pulls heavily on my heart. Before the kitchen, there's a scullery and, once inside, I barely say hello to them immediately asking to go outside and play pretend games with the pump handle. My imagination runs riot. In my fantasy world, I have a large family and need to draw water from the well. Inside, Small Grandma chats and laughs but Grandma is quiet. Mum says she suffers with her nerves. After our visit we can't wait to leave for Granddad's signal box.

According to Geoff Woodward, previously from Harpenden, our grandfather, Stanley Munt, was a man with a long service record who started as a porter at Wheathampstead and later went to Grimoldy, Lincolnshire, to train as a signalman. From there he was transferred to London Road, St Albans and in 1910 back to Wheathampstead, followed by a short spell at Ayot. He began working at Harpenden East in 1926 and worked there till he retired in 1958 at the age of seventy.

Granddad's typical Sunday was opening the signal box early in the morning and then going to a service in the nearby chapel. He returned to signal the afternoon train and, having seen it through, left to conduct first the Sunday school and then attend the evening service. To round off his day he went back to the box to allow the cattle train through at about 10pm and then closed up for the night. Work started again for him at around five o'clock the next morning. Apart from signalling, he spent many hours cutting the hedges and grass around the station, taking great pride in his 'garden'.

Norman Payne, of Harpenden, recalls visits to Granddad's signal box and in particular being present when Granddad received a letter from his second son, Hector, my father's younger brother, held in a Japanese prisoner of war camp. This was welcome news as there had been considerable concern, as it was well-known the Japanese ignored the Geneva Convention and treated prisoners of war badly. A neighbour had taken the letter to him at his signal box realising it couldn't wait for evening. Of course, many people received bad news such via a telegram which was brought by a post office telegraph boy on a bike.

Norman's father was Granddad's very good friend; they both taught in the local Methodist church Sunday school. Norman described my grandfather as his role model – a great man who worked tirelessly at the Batford Methodist chapel. One winter day, despite being in his eighties, when snow fell, he went to clear the paths around the chapel. Sadly, later that day he suffered a stroke and was taken to hospital.

On her marriage, my grandmother, Minnie Smith, was given two houses by her father, a builder of many Batford houses and the Lea Valley estate. They lived in number 30 Batford Road (also Royston Cottage), Harpenden.

A staunch Methodist, NUR trade unionist and Labour voter, our granddad believed grammar schools were elitist, so our father, despite being nominated by his teacher to take the examination at eleven, had not been allowed to do so. Granddad brought up both sons to go to the chapel, five minutes' walk away, three times on a Sunday but my dad never embraced Methodism. My parents marry at St John's church and my sister and I are brought up C of E.

He is waiting, leaning over the wooden rail of the signal box, smartly dressed in his British Railways uniform. The railway is the Nicky Line. On arriving home he changes into smart clothes for union meetings or going to chapel.

Granddad is alerted to a train coming by the token released in a cupboard and which he hands over to the train driver exchanging it for one from the driver, which was given at the previous station; this is all done while the train is moving through the station. The token gives the driver the right to drive the train on to the next section of track. If two trains need to use the same track, the driver holding the token has the right of way and the other train must wait. Granddad is house-proud and the interior of the signal box is kept clean and smart. He is always jolly.

We return home via Station Road passing the watercress beds on our way.

The track where my grandfather's signal box stands is eventually turned into a footpath and cycleway, now known as the Nicky Way.

1955

'But for those brave women,' my mother says, 'none of your female cousins, aunts, myself or your granny and grandma would have been able to vote.' She's talking about the suffragettes.

In 1918 the Representation of the People Act was passed which allowed women over the age of 30 who met a property qualification to vote. Although 8.5 million women met this criteria, it was only about two-thirds of the total population of women in the UK.

The 1922 United Kingdom general election was held on Wednesday 15 November 1922. It was won by the Conservative Party led by Prime Minister Andrew Bonar Law. Granny Weston was thirty-two years old and it was the first time she could vote. She was up early and dressed smartly as usual in her two-piece suit with a special hat for the occasion.

Mum uses the train to take my sister to and from her boarding school. I travel with Mum sometimes. For a mother who thinks education is the most important part of life, she is amazingly willing to let me have a day off school to collect my sister. I get excited about going up to London.

Mum has been travelling through London for years. In the war she had to run down to the Underground when there was an air raid. People slept down there during the bombing.

'We were lucky in Harpenden,' she says.

Apparently, Mum was told I would be less jealous if I am a part of my sister's journey to and from school. Granny comes sometimes. She likes to shop in Kensington or Oxford Street so after collecting my sister we take a bus to the big shops, buy things we need and go into the Lyons Corner House for lunch. Granny's treat! When we cross London on the Underground or use a bus we see black men and women working.

'From Jamaica,' explains Mum. 'They work there as they are not allowed in many jobs.' There are no black kids in our school. Mum says if we lived in London we'd have classes full of them.

Granny still visits when she wants to watch television. She likes Billy Graham who was on tour in Scotland after New Year and hopes to see him on the 'telly'. Mum doesn't like us calling the television, telly. Short names are 'common'. Nothing new there.

Luckily, Mum likes cinema. We've been to see the film *The Dam Busters* just last week. But for now she is going to vote in the 1955 General Election. It's the evening of Thursday 26th May and I am pestering her to tell me how she's going to vote. I am only nine years old but I know about Conservatives, Labour and Liberals. Mum says it's a snap election because Winston Churchill has retired due to ill health. Anthony Eden takes over as Prime Minister, television with adverts began and the first commercial channel was ITV. Mary Quant opened her first shop, 'Bazaar' in Chelsea, London.

'You should never tell anyone how you vote,' says Mum. 'It can cause arguments but you must vote as women fought hard so your generation could cast their vote.' Regardless of whether I show any interest or not on the history of the suffragettes, she continues, 'One even threw herself in front of the King's horse at the Derby in June 1913.' Some women were put in prison and force fed when they went on hunger strike.

My parents walk to St John's School to vote. I'm accompanying them in what I see is an unusual happening. My father often works late but, today, he is home early, washes and changes his clothes. His work clothes smell of leather. I am thrilled to be with them but also annoyed at having to stop playing in my den.

Neighbours are walking down Grove Avenue to the polling station together, the couples' arms linked in a sudden and unusual demonstration of their bonding. As one pair passes another they nod to each other as if to acknowledge the reason they're out.

Soon the election is forgotten. All the talk is about Ruth Ellis who is sentenced to be hanged on 13th July in Holloway. One of my classmates gets the telephone number of the prison and phones to argue for a pardon. Between 1950 and 1955 there were ninety hangings but Ruth Ellis was the last woman to be hanged.

Soon school holidays are here. It's summer. Today, we're in Westfield cemetery, tidying up Granddad's grave for my grandmother. When we finish Mum takes me to the children's cemetery, secluded behind the big hedge in an area with many small crosses. Betty Weston's grave is there, the daughter of Uncle Reg and Auntie Rose who live near the basket factory.

'She ran out in front of a car,' says Mum. 'She was killed instantly.'

Another day and the school holidays amble along. After playing in our tent on the back lawn, my sister and I change into our best dresses. A visitor is coming for tea.

While we wait, I read my Malcolm Saville book, one of the *Lone Pine* adventures. Saturdays in term time and any day in the holidays I cycle up to the library in Vaughan Road. Saville is a local author living at West End Farmhouse, Wheathampstead.

Our visitor arrives on the 321 bus from St Albans where she lives with her elderly mother. She and Mum worked together at W S Green, a well-known department store in Chequer Street, St Albans. Mum left school at fourteen and worked there for ten years before marrying my father. She attributes her excellent present or parcel wrapping skills to her training at Greens, tutting loudly at my untidy attempts each Christmas. This great friend is Marjorie Inwood, Marge to her and Auntie Marge to us. Unmarried and childless, her visits are a holiday treat. The friends chat for hours while we must be quiet, play games or read. On Auntie Marge afternoons Mum never notices what we are up to.

Mum and Auntie Marge were working together when war was declared on Sunday 3rd September 1939.

Everyone was convinced Germany would invade England. Hitler had already invaded Czechoslovakia and Poland.

When my mother and her friend recall old times, I prick up my ears and listen. The gossip concerns people I barely know.

As well as getting family history from eavesdropping conversations, my grandparents tell me anecdotes about their childhoods. In particular Granddad Weston who had a colourful childhood growing up in a family of twelve children (eleven boys and one girl) on a farm in Topstreet Way.

When a cow was expected to calf, the boys would play a joke on their father. Great Granddad Joseph Weston was becoming rather deaf and he relied on his offspring to tell him when the cow let out a cry as she began to give birth. With no television to keep them amused, and little home space, sitting around the kitchen table was opportunity to make mischief. The boys would wink at each other.

'Hey, Dad, is that Bessie I can hear?' they'd say. He'd put all his outdoor clothes on and pull on large gumboots which required help from the children or his wife, sometimes both. After a protracted spell of donning the many layers of clothes needed in the cold weather, he would stagger out of the house to see to whichever cow he thought was in trouble. After 30-40 minutes he would return to the kitchen door grumbling it was a false alarm never realising the boys were leg pulling.

The War Years 1939-1945

Dad never forgave Hitler for having to go into the army immediately after my parents' wedding. Despite his reluctance and his resentment at their separation, he was a good recruit and soon promoted to instructor. The new rank meant less scrutiny and he often used a day pass to a nearby town to slip off for a romantic weekend. On these sorties, he hitched lifts to and from camp. Once, a military police vehicle slowed to offer a lift and he waited with bated breath, heart pounding. The police checked his pass but, unfamiliar with the geography of the area, the place name meant nothing and he was given a lift and then cheerily waved on.

Soon after my mother arrives back at her parents' home in Southdown, two London evacuees arrive. The Public Hall is used as an evacuee reception centre. Manland Primary and Secondary Schools are being built and, when completed, become reception centres. Children arrive with labels on their coats, their ration book and one small case of clothes.

While some resent these incomers, my grandparents, now known to their new protégés as Auntie Annie and Uncle Bert, are gentle and loving; they enjoy their presence and my mother amuses me in later years with tales of the boys' mischief. After the first months of what everyone called the Phoney War, some children drift back to their London homes, but the two boys stay put in Harpenden, happy to play on the Common and in the fields, making the most of the greenery before it's lost to potato and crop growing because the German U-boats have made sure Britain's food imports are sunk.

But as well as evacuees from London, Harpenden begins to see a steady stream of refugees. England accepts all refugees without questioning religion or political beliefs. Even Nazi sympathisers are admitted. England is a free country with no restrictions on views. One day when we are collecting my sister from Victoria, Mum takes me to Hyde Park Corner to show me the meaning of free speech.

Despite my parents hurried wedding arrangements, no bombs drop on our Village and the population don't see Germans march down Harpenden High Street. The months after September 1939 are quiet until May 1940. People become complacent and many homesick evacuees return home only to find to their cost the main blitz on London is about to start.

In May 1940 the beaches of Dunkirk are crowded with British forces pushed back to the coast by the German Offensive. Many small motor boats from remote inlets around the British coast heroically risk bombs and gunfire to speed across the Channel and ferry troops to larger ships waiting offshore. My parents and other families are able to see film of this on the Pathé News in Harpenden cinemas. This is before television and going to the cinema is a popular pastime. Pathé News, with its familiar music and the crowing cockerel, appears between the main feature film and the B movie, the supporting film. Other than dance halls and weddings, cinemas are the main source of entertainment and the foyer is festooned with red carpet and extends up the stairs, used by cinemagoers with enough money to pay for balcony seats.

My father as an instructor escapes active duty. Others are not so lucky. Our Auntie Marge, sadly loses her brother who is only eighteen years old. He trained in the RAF as a pilot for bomber crews. One night, in the early years of the war, his plane failed to return with no trace of plane or crew. It was assumed the plane, full of bombs, was hit by anti-aircraft fire.

As there are now no imports from overseas via ships, the large gorse-covered Common in Harpenden, the town's pride and the reason it retains its Village status, is razed and ploughed over in order to grow crops such as wheat and barley. Also anyone who has some garden grows their own vegetables and large DIG FOR VICTORY signs appear all over Harpenden. People are encouraged to dig over their lawns and grow potatoes.

However, in early 1945, with the war's end in sight, a general level of optimism seeps through the country raising the birth rate. I am one of the first baby boomers and, with a September birthday, my schooldays are marked by being the eldest in the class.

When my mother is pregnant in 1945, a three-bedroomed house costs about £1,320. A newspaper is 2d (about 1p today). Old money means there are twelve pennies (12d) in a shilling and twenty shillings (20s) make a pound. In September 1945, a pint of beer is 11d (just under our 10p coin) and a newspaper is 2d (about 1p). King George VI is on the throne, Clement Attlee is Prime Minister and Winston Churchill is Leader of the Opposition. Mum is one of Churchill's greatest fans.

1953

I watch as my father shows an endless stream of visitors, neighbours and family members around his garden, a composition of creative genius built from scratch. He patiently guides them along the paths which surround his lush vegetable and fruit patches, occasional fruit trees, particularly Conference pear, and his cold frame where he nurtures seeds and small plants before planting. As they walk, he's explaining his *raison d'être* for each plant.

My dad digs over a piece of garden for my sister and me while dispensing brief gardening hints and mantra. We grow tomato plants, flowers from seed, lettuces. I grow radishes every year as they bring quick results. I have a little path down the middle of my garden made of stones. It saves walking on mud. I water my sister's plants for her as she's away at boarding school to, although sometimes her plants thrive more than mine. Mum says I fiddle too much, digging about in the earth to see if the seeds are growing.

My father grows lettuces under cloches (curved Perspex or glass hoods put over the plants). Some are set into the ground. This ensures growth is staggered. Every spring my dad digs the vegetable patch over. He also hollows out trenches and loads compost inside for the runner beans. He uses the wheelbarrow to transport the manure further down the garden and, when empty, I am given a ride in it. The garden is a tremendous source of pleasure. Everyone makes approving noises and congratulates him on his green fingers. My sister's friends who stay at half-term remember my father for his gardening skill. Rows and rows of cabbages and spinach expand behind the rockery. Lines of lettuces sprout to feed Daisy the tortoise. The hedges are thick and leafy, the lawns, carefully sown from seed nurtured and taped off to prevent children's damaging footsteps. He takes no chances. Seed catalogues arrive daily in late winter and I never see him buy a plant. He gives away many he has grown.

In this garden, Dad is lost to the stresses and strains of work and family life which is often not as he would like. I am allowed – even asked – to pick loganberries from the canes on a Sunday morning for loganberry crumble and I stir the custard, often ruining it. Everyone is complimentary about Dad's fruit. Sometimes I pick gooseberries and Mum makes gooseberry fool but it's sharp to the tongue and doesn't contain enough custard. Also we can't afford cream. I promise myself my children – whenever I have them – will not have to eat crumble or lumpy custard.

The strawberry plants and raspberry canes are covered with net but the birds peck through and help themselves. Dad makes a scarecrow with a stick and some of his old clothes. When we are able to afford bought cake we save the foil containers and Dad makes a hole in each and strings them across the fruit bushes. One of my jobs is to water the runner bean flowers to make them set. I know my jobs and I do them before Dad has even left work. He arrives home to be told it's all done and he congratulates me.

At the end of the garden path, a rabbit hutch built by Dad and placed on wooden stilts to keep predators at bay, houses a few generations of rabbits during my childhood. They eat the outer cabbage leaves, outer lettuce leaves and spinach. Potato peelings are saved for making mash and I buy bran in the village pet shop on a Saturday to add to cooked peelings. Dad likes me to have a rabbit as I clean the hutch each weekend and put the droppings on the compost. The compost pile stinks. I wonder if the neighbours groan amongst themselves when they are down wind on a hot day.

Next to the hutch there's my play space. I collect broken runner bean canes that Dad no longer needs and hessian sacks from coal deliveries. I build a den, a house large enough for me to stand in. An old stool and table are used for writing my stories. This is my normal but later I discover not all children write.

In the distance I hear Mum calling and make my way back to the house but I have not heard the earlier calls and I am berated for dreaming. My dinner sits half cold on a plate.

My den is a haven for quiet reading. I also have a wigwam which, when pitched on the lawn in hot weather, provides seclusion.

Outings

Going blue belling is a spring treat. A plethora of woods, farmers' fields and public footpaths provide access to the bluebell woods. We cycle everywhere, pull bluebell bunches rather than cut them bringing them home in newspaper, protruding from our saddlebags.

In those days we pick wild flowers indiscriminately, the word 'environment' not yet in the dictionary and flowers multiplied prolifically unaffected by car pollution.

In later years the wooded areas are reduced and farmers and other landowners sold land for building but there were strict Green Belt policies in Hertfordshire.

A favourite outing is to Nomansland usually for a Sunday afternoon picnic. We cycle to the bottom of the road, and left into Grove Road to a farm track which leads to the Common near Wheathampstead. My sister and I wander off to explore the thousands of paths on the common. At weekends there are cricket matches on Nomansland and many people picnic on blankets near enough so they can watch. We don't. We're not into the cricket.

The foundations of Grove Road were built by German prisoners of war (POWs), imprisoned in Batford Prisoner of War Camp. They collected the potato crop on the Common during the war and, in the very bad winter of February 1947 they worked for the Urban District Council, shovelling snow from paths and roads. Befriending these prisoners was forbidden. An anti-fraternisation law was easily enforced due to revulsion about the atrocities in the Europe concentration camps and the estimated six million Jews sent to the gas chambers.

Along Grove Road, we see the prefabs, where people bombed out of their homes in the London Blitz are temporarily housed. Prefab (short for prefabricated) were built of a mix of concrete panels and corrugated asbestos roofs. I hear a well-spoken woman tell my mother, 'No-one would ever understand how we came to be here.'

At the time I find this mysterious. However, while some people made money in the war, many others lost homes, valuables and money – in fact everything. Those wounded in the war were later unable to work and there was no unemployment or housing benefit. The prefabs were later replaced with a small housing development.

Beyond the prefabs, Grove Road was a dead end. In the early 1960s, houses are built and the estate is named Paddock Wood. However, the green belt beyond remains to this day.

One day we cycle as a family to Ayot St Lawrence. When we arrive we find we are at George Bernard Shaw's house. I'm told he was a writer so show obvious interest. I learn he wrote several novels without success, but his later plays ensure he becomes a well-known writer and proficient speaker. His house was known as Shaw's Corner and was his home for over forty years, Shaw's Corner is a 1902 Arts and Crafts house set in a quintessentially English garden. It feels like Shaw has just left the room, from the clothes in his wardrobe to the typewriter and glasses on the desk in his study.

Some weekends we go fishing for tadpoles and minnows. We cycle up Cravells Road or Walkers Road, then to the A6 and on to Beesonend, our nets fixed to the backs of our bicycles and, in our saddlebags, empty jam jars, their lids punched with holes to provide air. At home, we put them in an old tin bath relegated to the back garden which Dad tops up by a small length of hose on the kitchen tap, for filling the watering cans.

Soon, the tadpoles disappear and later we have frogs hopping around the wet lawn.

November 1953, 8 years old – A Piano, A Gramophone and Some 78 records

I always have a soft spot for Granddad Munt as when I am seven or eight years old he does something which changes my life. He arranges for the piano my father used as a child to be sent to our house.

And so one fine day, an upright mahogany piano is delivered and wheeled, with great difficulty, into our sitting room. It is placed next to the fireplace and, soon after, I am whisked up to Milton Road, an area known as Poets Corner, for lessons. After a few lessons, I gather she's traditional and overly strict, her aim for all pupils to do high grade examinations. Even at the tender age of eight I sense tension and feel a shift inside my stomach each week. I hate exams.

At home, I plead I only want to learn for private amusement and not for strange examination pieces. No doubt my mother paid for a full term and the fees are forfeit but nothing is made of the fact and the lessons cease forthwith.

One day Mum hears of another piano teacher in Hollybush Lane. So every Wednesday I walk from Manland to my dad's shop, collect my bicycle and cycle along the

Lower High Street (supposedly safer), to Hollybush Lane. I have lessons for eight years until I start college. These are some of the happiest experiences of my young life. An enthusiastic pianist who can play by ear, she entertains me with jazzy pop numbers with a strong beat using her wide portfolio of show music. She taps out catchy songs such as 'In the Mountain Greenery'. Through such popular pieces, she inspires a love of emotive classical pieces such as Beethoven's 'Moonlight Sonata'. By the time I leave her tender clutches I have a sizeable repertoire of classical and popular pieces.

I nickname her Miss Thumper. She quizzes me on my favourite music. I'm now listening to Granddad's radio – a large cabinet – which stands on my bedroom dressing table. Miss Thumper – actually she is married – shops for sheet music that will appeal to me. Nothing is too much trouble. Before I learn a piece, she plays it several times and I stand alongside singing my heart out. I am then taught the piece line by line and phrase by phrase, Miss Thumper modelling each line first.

Granddad shows great interest in my piano progress.

'What are you learning to play at the moment?' He's arrived for his first Christmas visit since the piano arrived. He asks me to play certain pieces – his favourites. He listens intently, his face beaming with pleasure. Later, I learn songs and 'Wouldn't it be Loverly' and 'Winter Wonderland' become party pieces.

I'm sure it's his interest and encouragement that ensures a love of singing and piano playing. Later, I join a range of choirs, eventually joining the local musical theatre company in Swanage performing in *Guys and Dolls, Hello Dolly, Pyjama Game* and *Annie Get Your Gun* and more.

And then ...

'The fairies must have brought it.' Mum is dismissive of why a gramophone has appeared in our sitting room. There, as if by magic, is an HMV (His Master's Voice) wind-up gramophone and some 78 rpm records in a large brown case, the rpm related to revolutions per minute. HMV's symbol is a picture of the dog, Nipper, from the original painting by Francis Barraud, ARA of a dog listening to a cylinder phonograph.

Some are scratched and need encouragement via a finger flick on the needle arm. Old song books also appear with traditional, rousing tunes such as 'Goodbyee', 'Who Killed Cock Robin?' and 'Molly Malone'. I suspect these come from my grandmother, whose own love of music and singing endures the music ban imposed by my mother in 1943 on discovering my sister was deaf. The following year, my annual Christmas concert for the family includes dancing and singing to songs on the old vinyl LPs.

While all 78 records sport the picture of Nipper listening to the music, our gramophone does not have this attachment, being slightly newer than the one pictured. These belong to my mother and my father long before their marriage and comprise *Viennese Memories of Lehar and Strauss*, some Gilbert and Sullivan operettas and other rousing patriotic singalongs. I quickly learn the words and the tune of 'Land of Hope and Glory', 'Rule Britannia' and 'The Sailor's Hornpipe'. Later I incorporate the national anthem, 'God Save the Queen', insisting everybody stands.

Each record is carefully lowered by an arm, with a stylus – needle – on to the Bakelite disk. Any sudden movement scratches the records and those already damaged hiccup a word or a line over and over again – what we call stuck in a groove – usually to great hilarity. When blunt, the needles are replaced. Spare needles are stored in the gramophone's lid.

After the piano's arrival and enthusiastic recounts of my piano lessons, I'm treated to a Saturday matinee performance of the local Operatic Society's performance of a Gilbert and Sullivan opera at the Public Hall.

This introduction turns me from a musical ignoramus into an aficionado and I still sense frissons of excitement ripple through my body waiting for the curtain to rise on a musical or play. From the start of the overture I am in seventh heaven.

I go home and learn the songs. I dream of being a leading lady but I am too young and, even when old enough, I lack opportunity. When I'm sixteen, my mother's encouragement has strict limits. It's made clear one late night home from my piano lesson is enough distraction from schoolwork and revision. Sadly, even my piano lessons cease as priorities change.

This operatic debut – *Ruddigore* – means trips to the Harpenden Operatic Society's performances become a regular event. Now aware of the wonderful music, witty lines and ditties of Gilbert and Sullivan, the records in the large brown case suddenly hold more interest. There are several G and S records, namely *HMS Pinafore*, *The Pirates of Penzance*, *Ruddigore* and *Yeoman of the Guard* contained in its deep dark depths. The gramophone crackles and hisses. I select favourite pieces and incorporate them into my concerts, although I often mishear the words. Usually, my mother can enlighten me.

At school I clown around. I change the words for other hymns and songs to the common version as I urge my classmates on While Shepherds Wash their Socks by night, all seated round the tub …

I even persuade my form to raise their feet when we are being taught to sing 'As did Those Feet, in Ancient Time'. All fifteen members of the front row in our music lesson co-operate with an exasperated newly-qualified teacher pretending not to notice.

I doubt Mum was an angel at school either as she only has to let slip that as a schoolgirl she changed a line, for me to encourage classmates to sing, 'Just as I am without one flea!'

Innocence is splashed across our faces.

Acting About, 1954

'Roll up, roll up, come to the show.' This is me at about eight years old preparing to entertain our relatives on their Christmas visit.

Most of our day-to-day family activity takes place in the living room, a kitchenette and dining area. Here I have my hair washed on a Friday night and curlers or waving combs are wound up in my hair so when it's dry I resemble Shirley Temple.

'Shirley Temple,' says Dad, 'was a child actress when your mum and I were going out together. We went to see *On the Good Ship Lollipop*.'

My sister has naturally curly hair so she's spared this painful ritual. During the war my mother had, on hair washing nights, wound her hair in pipe cleaners, after which her long auburn hair would be dried, sitting up against the fire and later combed out whereupon it was full of frizz. This Friday night fireside hair drying continues until we acquire the novelty that is an electric hairdryer.

The wide use of the living room leaves the lounge, which my parents call the sitting room, mostly unoccupied, unwelcome in winter cold but useable in summer heat when temperatures are higher or when my mother or father light a fire in the grate. At one time coal is used but later my parents discover Coalite, a smokeless fuel, which provides intense heat with red glowing balls and an absence of flames. Often, to enable me to do my piano practice in the sitting room, my mother switches on one bar of a recently acquired portable electric fire. This is also used first thing in the morning downstairs during breakfast and in bedrooms prior to going to bed. We carry it from room to room.

Once the sitting room is warm, I disappear into its depths for solitude, to play the piano or prepare my show. I devise complex programmes with folded drawing paper and my rather inartistic and paltry decorative attempts on the cover. The scene is set around and behind the floor-to-ceiling curtains at the garden doors. Inset between two shoulder-height windows, the door recess provides a back stage area and the two window sills, ideal positions to leave props lined up for use during the show. A chair is used behind one curtain to force some space for behind-the-scenes manoeuvres.

I spend long periods in this sitting room listening to records and assessing the suitability of tunes and songs for my concert programme. I discover more songs on 78 records and remember seeing these performed either at school or possibly on television.

On the evening of the concert, I use the small brass hand bell, from the living room fireplace, to act as the summons to the sitting room for all relatives at 7 pm. Numbered tickets are handed out at tea-time amidst much apparent delight, now seen realistically and, with hindsight, as patronising, yet polite, amusement.

The ceiling lights are switched off. The stage lighting is provided by a standard lamp, operated by my hand appearing around the floor-length velvet curtain and fumbling for the switch. Once the curtain is lit up, I make my entrance and announce the programme, despite the fact that it's replicated on several folded programmes handed out to family members entering the room. I have worked continually on the uplifting songs 'Rule Britannia' and 'Land of Hope and Glory' – all excellent and salient preparation for *Last Night of the Proms* in later life.

My singing is accompanied by energetic marching movements up and down the fringed edge of my parents' Indian carpet as I arouse my own patriotic fervour while my scabby and somewhat dirty knees are revealed from beneath an outfit of old costumes or discarded clothing cobbled together with string or pins. For 'Rule Britannia' I devise a flag made out of a small cane and the Union Jack painted on paper and bound together with tape.

Various musical items selected earlier are played at appropriate points in the show. In line with cinemas and theatres, the national anthem is always played at the beginning of the show when all present are obliged to stand to attention.

Another year – they are usually Christmas events – I put on a puppet show by fixing a string to many cracker and lucky dip toys I have collected over the years. I use a cardboard box turned on its side and material remnants from my mother's sewing machine are stitched over string or strung across the front opening to form curtains, a box flap being painted for scenery and new pictures clipped over the top when the scenery changes are required. As my artistic talent always leaves much to be desired, these pictures no doubt amuse the audience although they generally sit politely and clap at appropriate times.

My writing hobby also comes in useful when devising the scripts for these rather strange puppets. I give my sister a copy of the script so that she doesn't feel left out. I write them myself and use various accents when telling whatever story I am performing. However, more time is taken unravelling tangled puppet strings than performing, as I can never fathom how to store these puppets successfully.

One morning I come down to breakfast to be told by my father that there's a surprise for me in the sitting room. A surprise! I don't have many of those. On opening the door I spy something I never dreamed I might own. It's my very own puppet theatre together with curtains operated by a side pulley and lights which can be beamed down to various positions on the stage. I am intensely moved by this gesture and it makes up for all the cheaper presents I have been given over the years. Forever grateful and inspired by such a real theatre, I spend many happy hours making puppets, writing shows and performing before the toy theatre is finally relegated to the loft.

The puppet theatre has been designed for me and this makes it even more precious. My dad said he made it as a reward for investing so much time and effort in providing such puppet performances. It's not the first time my father has acted this way. A great lover of leather, he makes us napkin rings out of odd scraps and we all have our own colour. A sweet scent of leather lingers on our hands when we use them. When we are bigger he makes Susan and me a table tennis table to go over the top of the dining table. This is marked out and sized accurately for professional table tennis and is in two parts which joins at the centre under the net, painted green with white markings. It's stored in the garage and brought in on wet afternoons in winter half terms and at Christmas. My father is talented and never does things by halves. He has, no doubt, been to look at a proper table tennis table, taken in the visual aspects, written down measurements and carved it to that specification.

My sister is good at all sports as a child and young teenager so I always lose any game of table tennis or tennis that we play. The table is brought in if we have young visitors, particularly teenagers. My cousin sometimes comes to play table tennis but his main aim is to whack the ping pong ball as hard as possible in my direction.

In fact, many of the toys we have as children are made by my father. Some of these are of complicated design such as the doll's house, made for Susan when he was posted far away serving in the war. There was a shortage of materials and no new toys came into the shops as all resources were requisitioned for the war effort. However, my father, always ingenious, goes scouting around the base where he is stationed and in local towns and factory areas. He finds off-cuts of wood going to waste and sets about collecting these and turning them into the wonderful doll's house we enjoy as children. There are cords for the curtains, an upmarket way to open the drapes. The furniture he carves out of unwanted wood scraps. These items are replicas of pre-war furniture. Finally a battery in a roof space supplies lights to all the rooms. This toy is quite exceptional and, if a friend comes to play, they express surprise at the sophistication of this perfect replica of a 1930s house.

Please Pass the Sick Bag — 10 years old, 1955

Mum tells me I am lucky to go on school outings. She and my father never had the chance. Lucky them! My school trips involve coach travel which means sickness. I am the world's worst traveller. Today's school outing is our last before our eleven-plus year. It's to a historic site, the reason now a blur. I sit on the onward journey with a sick bag clutched close to my face. Usually I am the only one holding a bag. I know one or two other pupils in the school who suffer travel sickness but not in my class … until now.

Yippee! Today, there are three of us retching and heaving down our gymslips or simply sitting quietly in the front row hunched, white-faced!

Over the years Mum has collected a tranche of travel sickness remedies, tested out on bus and car journeys. Nothing works. The chemist gave up years ago. But there's hope! This morning, my mother has brought me briskly to the coach with a large pile of newspapers tied up with string. My cheeks burn with shame.

'This is a proven remedy for travel sickness,' she announces to the surprised teacher in charge. It prevents the engine vibrations coming through the seat and upwards to the stomach. She repeats the gory details to the coach driver whose eyes fill with horror. His coach is his pride and joy.

And so it is that I'm required to sit astride and on top of this expansive wad of papers at the front of the coach just behind the driver on the aisle seat. Despite the wodge, I am inert within ten minutes. Breakfast was safe but last night's dinner is ready for the off.

The front of the bus is, of course, near the engine, so one feels more ill, but the advantages of this position are, for those in charge, twofold. First, it ensures a nauseous ten-year-old doesn't bring up her breakfast down the erstwhile clean neck of a pupil on the aisle seats! Second, there's a slim chance that, at the point when a pupil's stomach contents are about to burst out, the coach may be in a position to do an emergency stop and the child ousted on to the pavement just in time and told to 'get it over with'.

I'm parked on pages covered with pictures of Princess Margaret and Group Captain Peter Townsend. Mum and Dad have talked of nothing else for weeks. The large newspaper bundle raises my position such that my head touches the overhead locker and, with no seat in front of me to hang on to, I bounce backwards and forwards freely in mid-air, sometimes sliding off the mound into the aisle as the vehicle, driven by an aspiring Brands Hatch winner, turns a corner. I am visible to sniggering peers and pedestrians who point in surprise at the sight of a girl appearing and disappearing with a scrubbing brush on her head.

As usual, I sit quietly, the pungent upholstery and engine fumes turning me a deeper shade of green. Wafts of cigarette smoke drift around. Smoking is yet to be pilloried by the medical profession, so the driver's puffs of tobacco eddy upwards and their effect on my nose causes involuntary retching. I try to ignore the window seat passenger with her nose in a bag. She has the window open and the summer breeze blows putrid vomit odour in my direction.

My friends at the rear are singing lustily. In any other circumstances I would be joining in or even leading the silliest or rudest of songs. This time 'Ilkley Moor Ba Tat' and the line about eating worms serve as a stomach pump.

Courtesy of my fussy mother, I have, in addition to last month's issues of the *Daily Express*, a supply of brown paper bags but even the pong of these makes me gag, especially the ones that previously held blue cheese. I pass one across the aisle to the third nauseated pupil and soon the coach develops into a vomit-scented fugue. I become the one whose stomach acts last, long after my nearby sick-mates have recovered. By the time I am heaving, they're stuffing their faces with chocolate or, worse, some sausage and piccalilli sandwiches, the sight and smell of which is, for me, the last straw.

Our visit over, we look forward to returning to the coach which, unventilated during our absence, bears a rancid smell and heralds pointed complaints from our peers. Despite this, I take solace from the fact that the return trip is usually more comfortable, there being no stomach contents left for a repeat performance.

However, today this is not the case. So relieved am I to get off the bus – I am ideally placed at the front to be first into the open air – that I race off down the stony path forgetting we are to walk in a sedate crocodile, and I fail to hear the final instruction, 'Don't run!' The words fade in the wind as I run faster and faster down the steep slope of rough gravel until my feet leave the ground. It's not uncommon for me to fall – I sport permanent plasters on both knees and elbows. Now here I am spinning down the hill and tumbling over and over, the brown earth turning to green and coming up to meet me face to face until I land finally in a large patch of stinging nettles. When I stand up, my legs and arms are a mass of grazes, cuts and large, white, swollen lumps. As the blood trickles down and seeps into my long knitted socks, I try to grin and bear it but the stinging pain wins.

My return trip without travel sickness should be a cinch but, instead, I am huddled in the window seat nursing my wounds and white nettle stings along with my pride. As our stinky transport stops at the Rose and Crown, I stumble down the coach steps and greet my mother who rather than seeming pleased to see me is deep in conversation with David's mother. Apparently Princess Margaret won't be marrying Peter Townsend after all. What a shame! Mum ignores my tearful face, the stinging now so intense I can think of nothing else. And there's little sympathy after my mother is told I hadn't heeded the warnings.

'You were told not to run!' My mother's tone is full of reproach. I barely need this reprimand as the stinging is punishment enough. The newspapers are forgotten and my queasy, sickly journey there and back on the monstrous school bus, is not taken into account. I howl as the cuts and grazes are washed and doused in antiseptic after which vinegar is slapped on the stings.

'That'll do!' She's brisk and brushes off my mishap with her usual sharpness. She doesn't suffer fools gladly and has an answer for everything. Her irritation is understandable, however. Unlike my sister, cousins and classmates, I frequently fall flat on my face and always have scabby knees.

That night I write in my diary, 'This was the worst day of my life.' How naive! Many years later after thwarted teenage crushes and more scrubbing-brush haircuts, this day is to look, not one of the best but certainly not the worst. If only life could be simple and a few grazes and nettle stings were all life throws at us.

Wouldn't everything be grand then, eh?

1956

'Look at you!' I jump as the words are hurled in my direction.

'What?'

'You have egg on your tie!'

I look downwards at my tie, cross-eyed. Sure, a blob of egg protrudes from my tie of royal blue and gold colours. Surely, a little bit of egg won't notice. At least I have eaten it.

Mum now has a refrigerator which some people call a fridge. She doesn't. It's slang apparently. At the top is a little box which is icy and yesterday she bought her first frozen food. I am yet to try it, these things called fishes' fingers.

It is no better at dinner.

'That cabbage has come from your daddy's garden.' Mum's pushing it to the front of my plate with her fork.

So what, I want to say, I still can't eat it.

Then I see my dad's face and his eyes refuse to meet mine. My stomach cringes and I burp cabbage goo back in my mouth. I mumble something about not feeling well but it's an old well-worn excuse and it doesn't wash. I really do appreciate his gardening efforts but, just now, I feel the most ungrateful daughter. He spends every waking hour when he's not at work on his vegetable garden. We're lucky Mum says. She reminds me she never has to buy cabbages or lettuces, runner beans or spinach. Oh yuk, spinach. I hate that too.

Mum's not the best cook in the world. I always enjoy visits to friends as the food is nicer. I am not saying Mum can't cook. She does but in her own way. And her own way was to prepare dinners with little effort, even less cost and without any imagination. She has Mrs Beeton's cookery book and when I am about nine or ten I like to try recipes out. I use the ingredients on the recipe but this doesn't go down well with Mum.

'Two eggs!' she exclaims. 'How'd you have been in the war, young lady? That's what I want to know' but I am spooning the mixture into the pate tins and really don't care.

Isabella Beeton's *Book of Household Management* rules in many houses. Lunch as we know it hasn't existed before the 1950s, as whatever labourers or mothers and children eat in the middle of the day doesn't have a name. It's Mrs Beeton who introduces the notion of dinner at the end of the day. Previously, we have school dinners at school and then tea or supper at home in the evening. Once she establishes evening dinner, a word is needed to explain what people and children eat in the middle of the day. It's Mum who finds the word lunch originates from munching or 'nchun leading to luncheon then shortened to lunch.

The name of the cookbook is shortened to *Mrs B*. It contains 2751 entries and, includes tips on how to deal with servants' pay (chance would have been a fine thing says my mother), children's health, how to do laundry, etc. While it's probably relevant in 1861, when it's published, few people have servants in 1950. After marrying Samuel Orchard, a publisher of books and popular magazines, Isabella begins writing cookery articles for this market. These are eventually brought together in her book.

My mother is not creative and she dishes up food on a plate in a heap – one vegetable plonked on another – without attempting to make it look attractive. There are no roast potatoes and only vegetables from the garden, served plain, with no butter on the mash and cabbage. Do you think we're made of money? Butter is a luxury not seen in our house. I only see it at friends' houses. Mum makes no pretence of her dislike of preparing family food. Subsequently, when describing the highlights of our childhood, neither my sister nor I would mention the food. That is except for suet dumplings and swimmers.

I love the weekly roast and Sunday lunch is beef, lamb or pork with vegetables from the garden. My mother jokes Dad doesn't know the difference between the three meats and blames it on his chain smoking, which, she says, affects his taste buds.

It's important to be economical after the war. My mother saves the fat from the roast for dripping and we are often given bread and dripping for tea. Mum can make a good casserole but she doesn't experiment much otherwise. In fact, she likes to spend as little time in the kitchen as possible. She even finds Sunday roast dinners tiresome. Our pudding is rhubarb or apple crumble and sometimes we just have apples and custard. From quite a young age, I look through Mum's *Mrs B* book and choose something to make, often cakes or pastry tarts, etc.

That's when I learn that eggs are used in cakes!

Many foodstuffs are only available in season and mostly we eat what comes off the garden. My mother has strict instructions from my father as to where in the back garden she can cut a cabbage or spinach. But I do have favourites – bubble and squeak with left-over potatoes and cabbage is one. At Christmas we have chicken, a real treat. The next day the chicken bones are boiled up with vegetables to make chicken broth. If we are ill, Mum gives us drinks of hot Bovril and we begin to have tinned soups, namely Heinz, particularly tomato – a favourite, dished up regularly by my grandmother.

Another popular meal is onion and bacon pudding. Mum has a number of cloths which she uses for suet puddings. Sometimes they contain jam, sometimes treacle – they are my favourites but the bacon and onion pudding is a pet hate. I push it round my plate with a fork trying to hide it under potato. The suet and flour mixture is rolled in flour and then tied in the steaming cloth. Afterwards, Mum boils the cloths.

Tastes in food are changing in the 50s and there is a British adventure into new dishes with Mediterranean ingredients but dining out is still a luxury. As a child, I never see pizza or pasta and there are few foreign ingredients available.

Sausages and casseroles are regularly dished up and sometimes we have toad in the hole made of either sausage meat or sausages cooked in batter. At other times we have sausages with vegetables and liver and bacon, sometimes made into a casserole. Other meals are stew, a cheap cut of beef or neck of lamb cooked slowly with vegetables for two hours. Mashed potato is in her repertoire but baked beans are a rare treat. I dislike salad but, when summer lettuces are ready we have to suffer both this and beetroot – another hate of mine.

If we have fish, my mother coats it in flour, fries it but never serves it with chips. When, at evening class, I learn to make a fish pie of steamed cod in a cheese sauce with hard boiled eggs, a treat that delights my mother. For the first time in my life I eat fish.

Reading and Writing Goes Mad – September 1956, 11 years old

It's Saturday and I cycle to the Village from Southdown. I have errands to run. I pedal furiously under Skew Bridge and past the Common until I get to the lower road. Once past the Public Hall and through a cutting past the Misses Gardners' cottage, I am in Station Road. Dad's shop is number 3. I wheel my bike into the back room and pop into the workshop to see what jobs Dad wants done. Sometimes he lets me serve a customer. He can see through to the counter so if he sees a nice lady he sends me to say, can I help you?

Next he gives me a pound note and a ten bob note (ten shillings) and sends me to Midland Bank on the corner of Station Road to get change for the till. He writes it down, 5 x 6d, 5 x 1 shilling, 2 half crowns. A half-crown is 2/6d.

Then it's off with Mum's shopping list to Sainsbury's where I have to queue for cold meat at one counter and then for cheese at another. Afterwards, I go to Leyton Road to Anscombe's to pay the club. I push the heavy door into Anscombe's and make my way through haberdashery. I stop to look in the remnants basket to see if there's some ribbon or braid I can use for my doll, but there's none today. I hurry through to the office, tucked away at the back of the front counters. I have Mum's club card in one hand and I clutch half a crown (two shillings and sixpence) in the other. The department store sells curtains, cushions, material, sheets, towels and small items of furniture.

The counter clerk uses an overhead cash rail system, the only one in Harpenden. The clerk puts the cash and card into a pot, replaces the lid and pulls a cord to send the money along a pulley system at speed to the accounts office where the card is stamped and the pulley system is activated to send it back to where I am waiting. Anscombe's club is a savings scheme. Once a year, Mum buys new linen with her Club Money. I like this errand; my favourite aunt works there and I always stop and chat.

As I near the shop door, I hear the bright cheery sound of my aunt's laugh and I turn. She's over in a trice hugging me hard and asking about school, my mum and dad and, believe it or not, my writing. No-one else is interested in my stories, other than Granddad. Most of the family laugh about it; my head is apparently lost in the clouds when it should be focused on school. Today she's asking me how the practice tests are going for the eleven-plus. I am near the top I tell her.

'Good for you,' she says, her face beaming.

'What's the uniform like?' she asks and I tell her.

My St John's Ambulance class is in a room that later becomes part of the library in Vaughan Road. Then it is back to the shop. My mother is serving customers, standing behind the counter in her nylon overall. It's busy so I am asked to do more errands. I am sent to Ackroyd's bakers at the top of Station Road, to buy a large homemade loaf. It's white bread with a crusty top. Also there's something to get at Boots and items from the hardware shop on lower High Street.

I walk back along the High Street and then go to the Public Hall if there's a Christmas bazaar. I buy clothes for the doll Granny gave me a year ago. If Mum is not working in the shop she takes me to Bunty's on lower High Street near Home and Colonial for tea and cake.

The library becomes my second home. For me books are a window on the world. Reading is a safe hobby that doesn't involve asking permission to go out or call for friends, something that's easily refused. Of course, in the 1950s there is not much to do.

One day I seek out *Swallows and Amazons*, and other Arthur Ransome books as an aunt has recommended these in advance of my interview for the grammar school. The *Lone Pine* books are also a favourite of mine. The author, Malcolm Saville, lived at West End Farmhouse, Wheathampstead. An avid reader of the *Lone Pine* Club, I visit the library each Saturday to borrow yet another in the series. He wrote twenty-one of these plus other children's novels, all often based on the area.

While I am a regular borrower at Harpenden Library, I am bought several books as a child. Two of these *The Children of Cherry Tree Farm* and *The Children of Willow Farm*, both featured town children moving to live on a farm, a fantasy after my own heart. I also had *Little*

Women, *Little Men*, *Good Wives* and *Jo's Boys* all written by Louisa M Alcott. The books are semi-autobiographical based on her life with three sisters. The Little Women are Meg, Jo, Beth and Amy. Jo is the writer, based loosely on Louisa and the one with whom I always identified. Beth is the youngest and suffers ill health eventually passing away. She's in love with their neighbour, Laurie, who, in the end, marries Amy. Meg is the sensible eldest daughter who marries Laurie's tutor in the first book. Other books in the bookcase at Grove Avenue such as *Little Women* and the other books in the series belonged to my mother. There was *What Katy Did* and *What Katy Did Next* by Susan Coolidge, the pen name of Sarah Chauncey Woolsey, books that follow the adventures of Katy Carr and her family, growing up in mid-western America in the 1860s. Katy, a tall untidy tomboy, is forever getting into scrapes while wishing to be beautiful and beloved. When a terrible accident makes her an invalid, her illness and recovery gradually teach her resilience. Two sequels follow, Katy as she grows up – *What Katy Did at School* and *What Katy Did Next*. Coolidge modelled Katy on her own childhood self, and the other Little Carrs on her brothers and sisters.

Finally, I own a copy of *Heidi* by Joanna Spyri, *The Secret Garden* by Frances Hodgeson Burnett and *Black Beauty* by Anna Sewell. Many of these books I keep and pass to my children and grandchildren. I use the books for make-believe game of Libraries and spend endless hours making tickets and fly leaves to put in the front of the book.

The rhymes of AA Milne remain jewels in my

collection. *Now We are Six* and *When We were Very Young* contain such wonderful and humorous rhymes which I read at length and I treasure these books to this day and read them to my grandchildren.

Comics were also available. I took two from around eleven, these put on my parents' paper bill with no argument. One was *School Friend*. The comic's 1957 Christmas Annual comprised a picture story 'Their Perilous Journey to Totem Hill' beginning 'Carol Wayne lived at Honeysuckle Ranch …' She often drove her grandfather's stagecoach on interesting trips to help the western folks. Imagine that these days!!

Another favourite was *Girl*, first issued on 2nd November 1951. Articles in the annual included how to write poetry, kitten care, instructions for an easy-to-make bracelet and how to knit yourself a ski cap. One story was, 'Anna learns to be a model' and other stories featured sensible girls (one blonde and one dark) who lend a hand and ride horses.

Children's stories in *School Friend* include children at boarding school sitting in their studies on sofas praising each other's work. They had adventures, adopted lost dogs, drove stagecoaches and experienced other exciting happenings. One story was set in Nazi-occupied areas in the North African Desert in 1942.

1956 – The Eleven-Plus and Grammar School

Grammar school selection looms. No extra tuition is needed with the excellent teachers at Manland. I am so keen I take extra work home. All my classmates take the exam in January but, out of fifty children, only half pass to grammar school.

When not beavering away at workbooks, I sing to Elvis Presley's 'Heartbreak Hotel' on radio and, in April, teary-eyed watching Grace Kelly marry Prince Rainier in Monaco on television. In May, we watch the first Eurovision Song contest. In July, my parents talk about nothing but President Nasser nationalising and blockading the Suez Canal. In October, Israeli forces invade Egypt with the UK and France following. It's over by November.

We watch TV news although at 6.45pm Mum insists on listening to the *Archers*. In the morning and repeated in the afternoon is *Mrs Dale's Diary* and my father is always joking about Mrs Dale saying she's rather worried about Jim, which seems to happen in most episodes. Mum also listens to *Workers' Playtime* every morning too and on washing day she sings along.

Mum and Dad love nature programmes such as *Away From It All* when Chris Chataway interviews farmers and shepherds in faraway places such as the Welsh mountains, the Lake District or Cumbria. It's the nearest they will get to seeing such places, although when I am fifteen we have a week's holiday in a caravan in the Wye Valley, my first holiday without my sister. We travel by train and bus. I miss sitting with my sister but she has now left school and is training on the comptometer.

* * *

Mr R flies into the classroom, as if jet propelled, a pile of papers in his hand. It's the Friday test results; the agony before the weekend.

'This is the most important year of your lives.' He is shouting although the class has gone quiet as he enters.

'Jones?'

'Sir?' An immediate response is needed if the cane is to remain in the desk drawer.

'What, you stupid boy, are seven eights?'

The object of Mr R's derision hesitates, his eyes wandering up as if appealing to a guardian angel.

'The answer's not up there, Jones.'

My stomach flutters. The tension in the air leaves my brain inactive. What if I'm next?

'The answer, Jones, should be in your head. What year is this?'

'Last year, sir.'

'Yes, Jones. Do that in the eleven-plus and you won't

be following that bright brother of yours to the Abbey!'

'Yes, sir.' Perhaps he'll get away with it. I see the relief spread over his face. Who wants the cane on a Friday afternoon so you can't sit down at Saturday cinema? Not that Saturday films are on my weekend schedule. My mother wouldn't allow that.

We wait, standing by our desks with the contents in our arms. Everyone has stopped moving to pay attention.

Two names are called, the owners making their way to the top two desks in row A. The A desks are next to the window. Their occupants can afford the slight distraction of 1F ambling on to the field for a game of rounders.

My name is next. So now I know I am third this week. I take my place as Mr R passes that morning's test paper which I prowl through to find the reason I am in third place. My mother will demand the answer. Next is a friend of mine. That's good, I think, as we'll sit alongside each other all next week. Until next Friday when we play musical chairs again.

The four rows gradually fill up with everyone knowing their place in the class. Even to be number thirty-two isn't that bad in a class of fifty. Yes we are the Bulge – the baby boomers, the result of our fathers' homecoming from war service.

The list drones on with the disappointed and the exultant taking up their places. As the group of children diminishes, so do the smiles on their faces. It cannot be worse, can it, to be left until last or even the last three?

1957

'Grammar School swot.'

The words linger in my ears as I wander down Thomson's Close the next morning but what I find on the ground brings about a very different day to what I expect.

If a grammar school place had relied on artistic skill, I would definitely not have gone to St Albans Girls' Grammar School but would have been relegated elsewhere. Whether, with encouragement, any innate artistic ability would have surfaced sufficiently to equal my academic talents, I shall never know. This lack of talent is best kept out of sight.

I cast my mind dreamily back. I'm six and sit at the dining table with paintbox, jar of water and blank paper. I am without ideas and nothing ever looks like it should.

'You're like me,' says Mum, flicking her red hair that glints in the afternoon sun. 'I was never good at art! I couldn't even draw the back of a cat sitting on a wall.'

She returns to her pastry or washing up, or whatever is keeping her in the kitchenette. Monday is washing, Tuesday for ironing, Wednesday is bedrooms, Thursday for cleaning some windows or other jobs she does every few weeks.

* * *

To avoid being called the class swot, I play the class clown. One class is Art and Craft. Today I find a suspender in the gutter and pocket it for later use. I mull over the possibility of using it in a prank. Suspenders come off large corsets and clip to stockings. I've seen my granny struggle into her whalebone. The one I saw resembled an over-sized nappy pin only larger and it was the uniform colour pink – well in 1957 there were no other colours for underwear. The enormous clip and the stud protrude through ladies' skirts. In those prim and proper days such objects were referred to as private.

'It's my *down belows*,' says Granny when she comes in from the doctor's. 'You know where,' she adds.

I keep the suspender in my pocket until that afternoon, only showing it to one or two people. When we line up outside the art room I decide, on the spur of the moment, to slip the suspender into a paint tin in front of a cissy boy in the class. He's asking for it!

Today Mr F is dawdling, moaning about this and that, keeping us standing behind our chairs and I start to regret what I've done. But to retrieve the object would draw attention to it. I sense all might not go well. I'd thought I'd get away with the prank and hadn't thought of the consequences. The current Teacher's Pet, otherwise called the Art Monitor, had put out the palettes and trays of paint. Some would be better than others. Some tins would hold hard, cracked paint or little flakes. Everyone liked new unspoiled tins. I couldn't care less but I harboured the idea that my art might improve if the tins were good.

A bad workman blames his tools, was a favourite quip of Dad's. He believed anyone could succeed if they tried hard enough. I wasn't alone in dreading getting dried up tins even with my lack of talent. It could spoil the lesson finding you'd drawn the short straw on paint.

But for now we're standing to attention by our chairs.

'Good afternoon, Sir,' we chant in unison.

Then out of the corner of my eye I see the wimp lean forward to open the lid of his paint. My heart sinks as he opens the pot. Opening the tins before being told is strictly against the rules punishable with the cane. Once we have scraped the chairs along the floor noisily and sat down, Sir says, 'Open your paints.' For this reason I expected the great discovery to be at a noisy time. I planned to retrieve the item before there were repercussions and definitely not at a time when the room was quiet.

The boy was obviously desperate to get good paint. We're still standing in silence as the tin lid clinks open. At the sight of the woman's suspender the boy in the next place lets off a guffaw. He grabs the pot, holds it up to show his mates. Now everyone knows there is something funny in the pot. Noises of disgust fly around the room. Sir shouts and storms across the room.

As he approaches the desk he spots the contents.

'Who put that mm hrmph in there?' He hardly dares to mention the object's name.

'Not us, Sir.'

By now Sir's face is red.

'So who was it?' he booms.

A deathly hush settles over the classroom as pupils wait to see who will be on the receiving end of Sir's temper.

After what seems like forever, the boy I confided in that morning, puts his hand up and in front of the hushed class he speaks my name. There are gasps. It's unusual for me to be in trouble. I had not bargained on being identified. I make a mental note to get my own back. Soon. With that, I feel a tight grip on my blouse collar as Sir frogmarches me out of the class. Heck! I realise I am heading for the headmaster's office.

'You'll get the cane,' mutter my classmates as I pass, swept along by these huge hands. I am not entirely sure of the truth of their whispers. Girls generally didn't get the cane. I put on my hard face which I save for such occasions. There is no way I'll admit to being scared.

But I am.

Inside the head's room, my legs quiver and my stomach churns. He looks severe and stern although he's always smiley in assembly. Well, he is unless he's giving a caning in front of the school, the ultimate shame at Manland. Today, the head greets me with surprise.

'So, why have you been sent to me?'

I hold out the offending paint pot.

The headmaster peers inside and his face cracks slightly open with a hint of smile. Well, I like to think that.

The Head begins a slow gentle lecture. He reproaches

me for letting myself down in a year when I have achieved success in the eleven-plus.

'I hope you won't waste the wonderful opportunity you have,' he says. I should have remembered I am one of his stars so… am unlikely to be in trouble. Well, that was what I hope.

I shake my head glumly, wondering when the punishment might start.

'Perhaps passing to the grammar school has gone to your head.' It's a statement rather than a question. I realise this is true. I feel untouchable now I've achieved the goal my teachers and parents wanted. Passing to the girls' grammar probably had turned my head. Could it be I was actually … rather cocky now I'm in the top twelve girls in my year? No

wonder my parents were cock-a-hoop about my success.

I return to the classroom subdued but, undaunted and with my sense of humour intact. The next week in art, I'm in further trouble. This week's topic is our garden, so I paint exactly what I see each Monday – a washing line pegged out with brassieres and knickers, my poor artistic skills, for once, greatly improved.

As I show off my pièce de resistance, my classmates began giggling. It didn't take much to attract the attention once more of Mr F, who, after the previous week, was already alert to my mischief. Before I can paint over my artwork it's discovered. So, here we go again; another trip to the head.

'If you are sent to me again,' he says, 'you really will be in trouble.' That was enough to stop my pranks.

My parents, blissfully ignorant of my shameless behaviour, are proud I've passed the eleven-plus but they question me about who else is going to grammar school or to the high school. As both my parents came from old Harpenden families, they know many classmates and their parents.

I wasn't all bad. In some respects I did well in other areas of school life. In the last two years at Manland I played netball – centre or centre right – and could run, catch and shoot well into the net ensuring I was made captain. Manland had a large field for other sports in the summer term and boys' football in winter. In the summer term we have Schools Sports Day held at the nearby National Children's Home in Ambrose Lane. On a 300-acre site the home had transferred from the old premises in Bethnal Green around 1912/1913. They trained boys for work with apprenticeships and skills such as shoe repairing. The children from the home lived in houses of ten or twelve children with a housemother and staff and the houses were situated around a very large green – known as The Oval. Each year these grounds were marked out with running lanes and, after the initial rounds on our school field, we could be chosen to represent the school at the NCH.

Christmas and the final year at Manland. I'm chosen to sing and dance Gretel in *Hansel and Gretel* in the school concert. Helen Broadbent played the mother with my neighbour and classmate Douglas Element, the father and David Jolly as Hansel. David was very musical and played violin. We both sang and danced through our scenes.

David later went to the Abbey school and sometimes we walked from the bus together as far as Piggotshill Lane where our ways parted.

Always competitive, I collect and play conkers that autumn but by the following July, my passion is marbles. I win every game and am proclaimed Marbles Champion. Some marbles are exquisite. A younger girl, begged me to give her my marbles collection when I left primary school. As I'd begun to think I would be a bit above playing marbles at grammar school, I handed them over only to hear she'd lost all in the first week of term.

Easter 1957

'I've passed!' Of course, I was expected to pass the eleven-plus but hearing my mum tell friends and relatives and seeing my name on the result slip today gives me an unbelievable burst of *joie de vivre*. Around that time, Agatha Christie's *The Mousetrap* begins Britain's longest run on the West End stage and there's uproar when the Russians put a dog called Laika into orbit.

My parents went to the Board School in Victoria Road on the site which is now home to the library. They're both intelligent and can tell me anything. They understand my arithmetic homework my spellings and much more. Neither had the chance of grammar school. My father didn't sit the exam as Granddad Munt believed grammar schools were elitist. In fact, the opposite is the case. The grammar system allowed for more social mobility. I mixed with girls who, without the grammar school system, would have been in private schools. Also, thanks to the opportunity, I had a good career.

My mother, on the other hand, was allowed to sit the eleven-plus and *did* pass the examination. However, when she becomes upset at leaving her friends, little encouragement is forthcoming and her parents allow her to give up her place. My maternal grandparents, both offspring of local farm workers, have low aspirations, no role models and therefore, on leaving school, enter low-paid unskilled employment. My grandmother goes into service at twelve years old in the house where her older sister, Sarah, is cook. My grandfather, at thirteen, becomes a grocer's assistant.

So, this is the high spot for my parents and my grandparents. It begins when I am invited for interview with the headmistress, Gladys Dwyer. Mum contacts family members – several cousins have children at grammar school. At the time, I have a great love for Enid Blyton books but, before I go for interview, I'm advised not to mention her. Instead, when asked what books I read, I say Arthur Ransome books such as *Swallows and Amazons*. A few weeks later, around Easter, a letter arrives offering me a place and my parents are, quite rightly, proud. It's important to them and they emphasise the significance.

Mum writes to my sister about my success and she writes a letter home congratulating me. Granny also seems quite proud. For a while I am in everybody's good books.

Dad says there's nothing to be ashamed of in being working class and working hard for what you have. I realise later he's worried I'll be mixing with rich children. But he has great hopes I'll have a better chance in life through grammar school. After my offer of a school place drops on our front door mat, my dad is visibly moved.

He says, 'Make the most of your opportunities, you have a chance that I didn't have.'

***

My mother now has a cleaning job, for a lady in a smart apartment in a road near Sun Lane. When home from school I go with her – we cycle all the way – and sit reading my book while she uses the vacuum cleaner and dusts lots of posh ornaments. Some are silver and others look like gold but Mum says they are brass. One day when we get home she says, 'Work hard at your grammar school and you'll never have to clean for anyone.'

I'm not listening, I think it's a strange thing to say but I do remember … always.

Little do I know but my life is soon to change in many ways. While I see the transition to grammar school as a small step, and the possibility of going back to see old friends, keeping up with primary school friends and sharing experiences, this does not happen. The long grammar school days, travel and homework leave little time for socialising with those who go to school elsewhere. High school pupils are rarely on our bus. They get aboard in St Peter's Street, St Albans and by the time it arrives at Sandridgebury Lane it's full, the upper deck swarming with boys from the grammar school and the Abbey school which is considered a cut above others.

Soon after I start at grammar school, Uncle Charlie is taken ill and dies. Dad finds himself overburdened with work. He and my uncle had taken turns to serve customers but now Dad is serving customers and repairs are not getting done. It's decided my mother will serve in the shop. She also does small tasks such as bagging up and pricing the finished repaired shoes and, with her head for figures, she assists Dad with the accounts. Dad advertises for a workman and when applicants come for interview he gives them a test – some shoes to repair. He only takes workmen whose work is of a high standard and one man, from Luton, works for my father for eleven or twelve years, travelling by train to Harpenden every day, the station only a two-minute walk.

The shop now has a new look. My mother involves herself more in the business, ordering leather goods from suppliers such as satchels, briefcases, bags and purses and the Christmas sales are brisk. I witness her joy at a role outside the family home and I admire her work ethic. I witness my father expending energy on high standard craftsmanship and naturally inherit my parents' motivation and work ethic.

From then, until 1968 when the business ceased and the property sold, both my parents were absorbed with running the shop, employing staff, paying wages and keeping accounts. My mother loved serving customers, an occupation she enjoyed as a younger woman. Every Thursday evening they sit at the dining room table calculating the wages for the two employees. Each workman's jobs are entered in a book with the price charged to the customer. They earned commission and, in the fifties, were considered well paid. I would be sat doing homework, perhaps learning some French vocabulary or doing maths, sitting in the fireside chair, while my parents worked on the paperwork spread out between them. On a few occasions when my mother was unwell, Dad asked me to help him. He would sit with Table A and I would have Table B. Fortunately my maths is good enough to be able to calculate the tax and deduct it from the wages without error and I enjoy doing it.

1957 – Swimming

Up to summer 1957, I don't have a very good relationship with water. Splash, whoosh and plop might make someone's day but not mine. Vivid memories of school swimming lessons at Kimpton Swimming Pool spring to mind, unheated and uncovered, its shallow end a trap for reluctant goose-pimpled flesh on both school swimming lessons and family outings.

For me there's no sink or swim, only sink! My sister, of course, learns to swim early in life and her skill increases every summer.

For now, back at Kimpton in the holidays, I must change in the cold outdoor changing rooms with a door that's hanging off its hinges. Then there's the agony of the rubber hat. I'm already wincing at the thought.

'You must wear it,' says my mother, 'or you'll get your hair wet.'

As if there's the remotest chance of getting my hair wet? I am determined to keep the top half of my body well out of the water. I hate my mother pulling the hat on as the rubber catches my hair, tugs it dragging at the roots.

Eventually I'm allowed to put this hat on myself. Now, I am halfway down the steps at the three-foot mark, on tiptoes holding as much of my body out of the water as possible and screeching as slight water surges edge higher up my ruched nylon swimsuit. I shiver and shake, my teeth chattering and my sister is laughing at my scowl.

'If you just get wet you won't feel so cold,' says my mother. 'Get your shoulders under.' Then the worst advice is, 'Get moving and you will warm up.'

What rubbish. How can I immerse myself in ice cold, chlorine-laden water and come out the other side warmer. The very idea defies scientific sense.

And then the awful exercise when Mum pleads, 'Lie flat and I will hold you …'

So keen am I to avoid all water activity I even leap across the footbath and once on the poolside sit dipping my heels somehow waiting for inspiration and trying to waste as much time as possible.

My sister calls from the other end of the pool.

'Deena, come on, Deena, get in,' and once I slither slowly down the steps and wet myself up to my thighs, she shouts again, 'Deena, let go, let go.'

Not flipping likely! I'm never more reluctant. Not for me the happy shouts, jumping in, the races, the dives or the descent to underwater navigation that my peers enjoy. With breath held firmly in, I edge into the cold and wet. I'm always on the lookout for crazy boys who run and make an exhibition of themselves dive bombing – running and jumping, with legs akimbo. One sight of them and I turn away, cover my face and wait for that sudden rush of icy water landing on my warm skin.

I am shamefully the last child in my final year at

primary school to learn to swim – in fact, I never do, learning long after I leave despite weekly lessons in the summer term.

Throughout my stand-offs at the shallow end, I try to be invisible and concentrate on the spartan white emulsioned walls feigning deafness when urged by a teacher to hold rails, kick legs. I never get my top half wet if I can help it.

It's to take an August holiday, one month prior to my twelfth birthday, for the warm, salty, gently lapping sea at Sandown to enable me to thrash about unaided for approximately five seconds. However, once I conquer taking my feet off the seabed, this is hailed as a great achievement by my admiring parents. I'm then tutored in strokes by Dad who says, 'She can swim at last,' at family get-togethers. However, I still avoid getting my face wet holding my head out of the water.

Other watery events are no better. The holiday treat of the pedalo ride is further torture. Keen to embark, my enthusiasm wanes quickly, as my sister deliberately rocks the boat and heads out to sea injecting terror on me skilfully averting her eyes from my parents' panicking gestures.

* * *

Then there's the annual crossing of the Solent on the Isle of Wight ferry. From the moment it leaves my stomach churns, the contents gurgling and rising. I remain below decks, walking around impossible. Urged on deck for fresh air accelerates the inevitable. My mother produces brown paper bags but the lingering smell of its previous contents such as pickle stirs my innards to explode.

'Try to get it in the bag, Dinah,' says my mother in resigned fashion brushing the splashes and bits from her travelling two-piece.

Alongside pathetic attempts to stay dry in the shallow end I barely sit on the edge of the sea. My sister, a confident swimmer, will stray further out to sea than my parents like. Their impotence at being unable to recall her leads to trouble especially when she's a teenager.

Wear It With Pride! Summer 1957

'Shall I measure her?' We're at St Peter's Street, St Albans in the specialist school outfitters. Mum is surveying the list. We're not well off and the uniform is pricy but my parents make nothing of it. No holds barred where my education is concerned. However, horse riding and ballet? Well that's a different matter.

Goodbye gymslip and hello stylish skirt. At last, I will look the same as my classmates. The most expensive item is the blazer. It's my first and I am thrilled – I've always envied my sister's school uniform – but my heart sinks in seconds.

'A larger one,' demands Mum.

The man in the shop is surprised but returns with one large enough for two. It hangs down like an overcoat; the sleeves descend beyond my fingers.

'That's fine.' Mum's voice is clipped and sharp. You don't argue with Mum.

'It's too big,' I protest.

'No problem, I can fold the cuffs and put a few stitches in to make a hem.' That makes me feel better. Years later I note an overly large blazer is the sure sign of a new girl.

The assistant reappears with a small item. It's a badge which Mum later sews proudly on to the breast pocket.

Another novel item is the tie; gold with royal blue stripes. I love it taking great pride in putting it on each morning. In the afternoon, once off the bus and along Grove Road, out of sight of senior girls, I pull it halfway down my chest! The navy beret is obligatory. This too has a badge although more like a brooch or pin in the form of the school coat of arms. It is worn at all times outside the school gates.

My gym uniform is a concern. The list includes a hockey stick. I've only played netball at primary school. I am not too sure about hockey. My sister is an excellent hockey player who later plays for Harpenden. She gives aggressive demonstrations of an opponent taking the ball. She whacks my ankle. I decide I hate hockey.

Then Elsa says we must have showers after games lessons or PE. I dread the thought, because I'll be discovered wearing the obligatory white pants beneath my navy ones.

I'm glad the other eleven girls from Manland are going to STAGGS. At least I will know some girls. It's a long time since I was a new girl. No Brownie or Guide camps for me.

I wait for September with mixed feelings.

September 1957

This is where we get off. It's Sandridgebury Lane and my friends and I are travelling on the 321 bus from The Plough and Harrow. It's our first day at the St Albans Girls' Grammar School. Today we start at 10 am but tomorrow we will need to queue at 8.15 to get a seat. We in Southdown are the end of the line as the buses fill up in the Village.

A September birthday ensures I am one of the eldest in my year. So, within two weeks of starting grammar school, I turn twelve years old. STAGGS is an acronym – a new word for me – and twelve of us from Manland have earned a place. Mum and Dad have already been to a new parents' evening.

Apparently, my form tutor is just like our next door neighbour. She laughs a lot. That makes me feel better.

There are three Manland girls in each of the four entry groups. Now we sit in the assembly hall waiting to be called by our form tutor, another new concept. I am with Christine and Mary in 1K. As well as her loud laugh, she has a shuddering bosom and makes us feel comfortable immediately.

Apparently we have The Butler Education Act in 1944 to thank for this opportunity.

My school skirt, like my blazer, is too big and my excitement at escaping the gymslip is short-lived. It descends to below my knees but I can get round this. Once out of the house in the morning, I roll the waistband over three times and the skirt stays above my knees. I only unroll it as I approach our front door at 4.30pm or if I spot my mother cycling up behind me on her way home. She must wonder why the waistband is creased but never asks.

Order marks are new and tame compared to the punishments at Manland. However, they're entered on end-of-term reports, a closely scrutinised by parents and sharply questioned. In tutorial we have to go and report any order marks we have received for being late or not doing homework on time.

The beret has a toggle and for new girls, there's a grand initiation ceremony – usually by second formers – and before the first few days have elapsed an older girl will have pulled off the toggle. This procedure is referred to as christening the beret.

This new-style hat is a vital symbol and, without doubt, the most important part of the uniform. We are expected to wear it from leaving the school gates until we walk through our own front door. If a senior pupil sees anyone not wearing theirs they'll report them. There are four houses: Salisbury (green), Mandeville (yellow), Verulam (red) and Breakspear (blue). I am in Mandeville and we wear a badge the colour of our house pinned to our ties.

I keep the uniform rules religiously for two terms, after which I find I can flaunt them. Luckily, although my friends get off at the Rose and Crown in Southdown, they are not always on my bus. There's good reason for this. A procession of buses arrives at Sandridgebury Lane between 4pm and 4.30pm. The buses are crammed full of boys from the Abbey school and the boys' county grammar as well as high school pupils. You can always tell if someone has a crush on an older girl or boy as they stand back and crane their neck to see if their 'pash' is sitting upstairs. A fleeting glimpse can make their day. If they're lucky they might even get a place on the same bus. After two or three crowded buses, the 321 begins to arrive empty so chances of seeing heartthrobs are over for the day.

At the Rose and Crown, once away from the bus stop and over the crossroads, I reckon I'm safe. Any older pupils from school either turn left up Piggotshill Lane or right up Cravells Road. I walk along the path by the shops opposite Cravells Road and buy my favourite treat – a sherbet fountain – in Fulliloves – at the end of the parade. Sometimes if I have enough money I buy a gobstopper, so called because once it's in your mouth you can neither speak nor breathe. At other times I get sweet cigarettes – long white sticks with the end painted red to mimic the burning end of a cigarette. I hold them in my mouth pretending I am smoking. Sometimes, I splash out on bubble gum and I become expert at blowing large bubbles which reach the top of my nose and pop leaving the gum spread all over the face, something much disliked by my mother. Other favourites are spangles, refreshers and liquorice sticks.

Eating in school uniform is forbidden and flagrant disregard of this school rule warrants the dreaded order mark. However, few older girls live beyond Cravells Road, most of them walking up Piggotshill Lane. Jill is a second former but doesn't have the authority to give order marks. So I buy the sherbet fountain, check the coast is clear, whip off my beret and swig the sherbet through the liquorice straw.

Total rebellion!

Absolute heaven!

After a full day of hard work at school – and work hard we do – this is my special reward. In my five years at STAGGS, amazingly, I'm never caught eating in uniform or without my beret.

Christine and I are protective of Mary. She contracted poliomyelitis at six years of age leaving her left arm and the adjoining chest area paralysed. She wears a sling for her limp left arm which along with her left lung will never grow beyond the size of a six-year-old. In the early fifties the epidemic could be contracted via polluted sea or lake water and so, for this reason, I'm never allowed in the Silver Cup Pond. Fortunately, in March 1953, a polio vaccine is successfully tested on 160 adults and children.

Two girls in our form are Swedish twins, Anne and Eva Hallgren, from West Common Way, who excel at sport and academic subjects. In fact, if I'm not top in a test it will be one of the twins who has higher marks. They are not identical. Anne is blonde and Eva is dark. Apparently their parents are divorced, a source of fascination for the rest of us. Few of us have divorced parents, although Xana, who has a Russan father, lives with her aunt in Welwyn Garden City.

The desks in the grammar school classrooms are designed for two people, unlike the Manland single ones pushed together. Christine and Mary sit together. I sit alongside Hazel Hook who lives in Redbourn. Hazel and I then join up with Xana Heiseler, Anna Veale, Sally James and Judy Hallam. Our original Gang of Six hangs together for five years at the school. In break times we disappear to the back of the school and down the field to the far corner where we have a den hidden in a small copse of trees and bushes. We sneak items from home to make it cosy. It's a secret and other pupils often ask our whereabouts during break.

In an early music lesson, the music teacher, Miss Macey, auditions us for the choir. Both Xana and I are chosen. Anna plays piano – but she doesn't make the choir. I often sing solos at concerts or in special assemblies. Singing solos is terrifying but I grow to love it.

Every morning, we file into the hall for assembly and sit cross-legged on the floor – the choir at the front. The staff sit on the stage. Miss Dwyer steps up to the podium to announce the title and composer of a classical piece of music. A sixth former goes on the stage and sits at a large radiogram cabinet. She lifts the lid, takes the stylus moving it gently to the edge of the vinyl record. We listen in silence. This daily dose of classical music has long-term positive effects on our musical tastes.

Maddy Prior is pitch perfect and sings a top A for Miss Macey when asked. She – later of the group Steeleye Span, famous for 'All Around My Hat' – and Gill Freeman, my cousin from Piggotshill Lane, leave school at sixteen and go to Cornwall in an old car which breaks down as soon as they arrive. They live like hippies for about 3-4 months.

I can't imagine my mother letting me do that.

There are only female teachers. It's to be five years before a man graces the stage in assembly. Some teachers wear gowns at special events but otherwise dress informally. We spend our first day in our tutor group with Miss Kaye giving timetable sheets and dictating subjects to enter, the block and room number, the homework subjects for each day. A guided tour follows with a floor plan. The school has four buildings. Salisbury is the building that houses craft subjects and leads to the front entrance.

'Silence, girls,' Miss Kaye reminds us not to speak when passing through the entrance hall. A statue by Barbara Hepworth stands on a plinth. Buildings are linked by covered passageways so we can get to lessons without getting wet. The assembly hall is at one end of the entrance hall and at the other is the block called Mandeville. The next block is Verulam and finally Breakspear, where in the first year we are given hygiene lessons, a polite name for sex lessons. We have one lesson a week with the Bod – historically the nickname for Miss Rudkin. The Bod is named because she looks after our bodies both with these lessons and teaching games and PE. Now we know some people already have the monthly experience which some call the 'curse'. Similarly we learn the rudimentary principles of female and male development and the link to menstruation. It's a revelation to find out grown-ups don't do sex just on the two or three occasions it takes to conceive a few children. While these lessons give us plenty to talk about, other subjects are exciting after the simple English and arithmetic lessons in junior school. Changing rooms – even blocks – between lessons feels grown up. Biology in a science laboratory is a novelty and we gaze in awe at the bottles on the laboratory counters.

In the first year we have double cookery. The first term we learn to make sandwiches. Then something on toast. Another term we learn how to boil, starch and iron a tea towel. Mum is impressed and can't recognise the towel she gave me that morning. Then it's basic sewing – buttons, hems, darning.

While I thrive on the academic, the same cannot be said about physical activity! Physical education (PE) in Gym or playing field is worse than I expect. I shiver on the sidelines of the hockey games unsure when to run or hit the ball and I am terrified of the hard ball and stick. Usually sent to the wing, where I can't do much harm, I run up and down the edge of the field in the opposite direction to give the impression this is a clever tactic. My talent for netball now seems wasted although an occasional game lifts my spirits. At least I can now swim. The Grammar School Parent Teacher Association is fundraising for a swimming pool on the school site.

The gymnasium is my greatest challenge. I've rarely been to playgrounds with climbing frames and slides. I can't jump over the horse but run and grind to a halt. Sometimes I pretend I've miscounted my running steps and return to the back of the queue. Other times I run at the horse, make as if to jump, landing on the front grabbing its side with my legs dangling. Other times, if the teacher isn't looking, I miss the horse altogether but act as if I've completed a successful leap, run back to join the queue. My worst dread is the wall bars. While most classmates climb and turn somersaults on them, my fear of heights prevents me scaling them. My heart sinks when we're required to hang upside down on the bars. One new young gym mistress – possibly a student – insists I must try and she gets a girl to help hold me upside down on the bars. This seems to last forever, leaving me in abject terror of wall bars for life. To save face, I discover quickly that helping put out balls and hoops and tidying up is one way to avoid strenuous activity, especially if do it slowly. 'A helpful member of the class' is preferable on my report!

Summer 1958

Just before the summer holidays, we line up at the gym for examinations. Inside rows of single desks await. It's like the eleven-plus all over again. We sit in silence and a teacher stands at the front invigilating. These exams are designed to familiarise us with the later ones. When the teachers announce the results, I am top in one or two subjects and come second or third in others. Mum asks who got more marks, then says, 'But you are as good as her.' Second is not good enough for my mother.

There's much happening. Granddad Munt has retired from his signal box and I'm sad I can no longer visit in the holidays and pull the number 19 signal. It was the highlight of my holidays but no more.

The news is full of CND, something we call Ban the Bomb. The Russians and Americans are in an arms race and now have a nuclear bomb like those dropped on Hiroshima and Nagasaki at the end of WW2. It made the Japanese surrender but the Pathé News at the cinema shows a little girl on fire fleeing the blast. There's something called radiation which is dangerous. Television news pictures show mushroom shaped dust clouds.

Xana and I have a CND (Campaign for Nuclear

Disarmament) badges. I want to go on a march but my parents say no.

'Where does it start?' asks Mum.

'It's London to Aldermarston.'

'Well that's your answer. No-one's got time to take you up to London.'

I hear a song on the radio sung by demonstrators when they're on a march.

'Oh when the saints, go marching in, when the saints go marching in.' I'm practising when Mum is out of earshot.

My aunt pops in on her way back from WI choir practice on a Friday afternoon. Mum tells her about the CND badge.

'No harm in it I suppose,' she says tipping her nose in the air and giving a sniff.

They talk quietly so I can't hear.

I catch my aunt say, 'Well, you'll get this now she's a teenager.'

I have heard other relatives refer to the fact I'll soon be a teenager. This is a new word. Teenagers provide a market for music and other commodities that appeal to this age group. There are teenage magazines – a new phenomenon – and clothes and cosmetics – consumables new to the late 1950s. Unfortunately, Teddy boys give teenagers a bad name. They wear tight fitting trousers and shoes with pointed toes known as winklepickers.

'Don't even ask,' Mum says when she hears me talking on the phone to Xana about the march.

Another new event is the installation of an immersion heater. Uncle Frank, an electrician, does electrical work in our house. Dad phones and says it's time we had one. Apparently, now we'll have hot water even when we don't have a fire.

So the thought of a holiday in Sandown, swimming and the putting green in Rothamsted Park help the days and weeks pass.

September 1958

'Hurray!' The second form – not the babies now.

In the first year Xana and I giggle about the Bod's hygiene lessons and the picture of a cow on the board, supposedly representing our ovaries, tubes and the womb. Now it seems several of my form have started their periods but there's no sign for me.

We gloat over the babies – first formers – doing our share of pinching toggles off berets.

I love being a teenager. Some relatives roll their eyes and forecast a difficult period ahead. I want no trouble at all and I am even less bother when I discover pirate radio and disappear to my bedroom every evening.

My gang are all avid readers but none more so than Xana. A favourite is Mazo de la Roche, author of *Mary Wakefield*, a governess who went to America to teach the two children of widower Philip Whiteoak. Rennie and Meg, the children, had been spoilt by their bachelor uncles, Philip's three brothers. We devour the series of books about the Whiteoak family and Jalna, the house built by their grandfather after he emigrated from England to America. Mary Wakefield falls in love with Phillip and they marry and have four more sons, Eden, Finch, Piers and Roma.

I love history, tales woven around dates and facts. English is another favourite subject. In the second form we study Shakespeare. Then the novelty of French and this year we get penfriends. My older cousin is visiting her penfriend this year and then her French friend will return to stay with her. I am not sure I want anyone to come to stay with us. My mother is so embarrassing.

To take my mind off this I go to the cinema frequently. *On The Beach* by Neville Shute is about the aftermath of a nuclear war, eerie as no-one is left except survivors in a nuclear shelter. The film inspires me to keep my CND badge. When old enough, I shall go on a march and tell my mother afterwards.

My favourite task in English is analysis or parsing where we have to draw a diagram of the subject, verb and object of a sentence and identify adverbs and adjectives. We are all well-versed in deconstructing sentences and, despite groans, this is invaluable in later life.

February 1959

Now my mind is elsewhere. I am grieving, devastated. Buddy Holly is killed in a plane crash in the USA. He is one of my favourite singers on my grandparents' old radio. I have danced to 'Peggy Sue', 'Donna' and 'That'll Be The Day'. Can't believe there won't be more songs. He was only twenty-two.

The 321 bus service meanwhile is inadequate. Many workers going to St Albans wait at the Plough and Harrow. Buses are full while we stand from 8am until 8.50am with freezing toes. Late for school, we miss registration and creep into assembly already in progress. Some parents mount a petition for extra buses. But ... we Southdown girls continue to suffer. Another year of cold waits.

Eventually, the parents have had enough and in my third year a coach is laid on from outside Conrath's butcher's shop. As we speed out of Southdown Road we see Loretto College and high school girls shivering at the bus stop. At 3.45pm the bus waits outside the school to take us home.

Summer 1959

Hot weather and friends are working to earn some money. I'm wondering what I can do. Around this time Mum comes off the phone to tell me a boy from Harpenden working on a farm has died after the tractor rolled over on a hilly part of the field and crushed him.

But today she is on the telephone and I hear her side of the conversation.

'I am sure she would love to do that?' Ooo I think, I wonder what I am going to be allowed to do at long last. Riding? Ballet?

Perhaps the chance to watch *'Room at the Top'* with Laurence Harvey? Xana says there is sex in it and a girl gets pregnant. Wow, a dirty film but I doubt I'll be allowed.

My mother agreed some time ago I could have membership of Elliswick Lawn tennis Club. I go with my sister sometimes but she's too good for me and it's demoralising. But I have a partner, Mary Barnes, and we have been playing in the holidays.

'What?' I ask as Mum comes back in the room.

'It was Mrs Barnes.' I look blank then remember Mary. We're well matched and give each other a good game. Neither of us is better than the other.

My first thought is I am in trouble but no.

A girl has moved from Bushey into Mary's road. She's been at grammar school and now has an interview with our head, Miss Dwyer. She's anxious about moving to a new school. Mary's mother has asked me to tea and she's asking the girl and her mother too. She's called Gill and she is only two months younger than me.

Suddenly I feel mature and confident. I'll enjoy being her guardian and mentor. It's the end of August and only two weeks to my fourteenth birthday and the third form.

On Thursday I get on my bicycle and pedal up to the Village and out towards Kinsbourne Green. I turn left and get off to push my bike up the hill. I've never been to Mary's house before. How nice to be asked for tea.

Inside I meet Gillian and her mother, Mrs Holdaway, and Mary and I chat about how school life is organised. We explain the house system, homework, procedures, languages we speak. It's a fun afternoon. My friends' mothers are more easy-going than mine.

'Tell Miss Dwyer you know Dinah,' says Mrs Barnes, 'and perhaps you'll be put in her form.' Meanwhile I'm invited to tea at Gill's where I meet her brother, Robert, two years younger. Then it's time for her to come to tea with me.

After her interview, Gill telephones. She's been put in my form and, although I don't know it then my life will change forever.

September 1959

Third Formers!!

So here we are back in the assembly hall for Miss Dwyer's annual pep talk on recent successes – O levels gained, A level successes, university places and high flying careers. 'All you girls can do the same.' I'm not sure I want university. I'm keen to teach young children preferably seven- or eight-year-olds. Teacher Training is only two years – quite appealing to me. I love children and think I'd make a good teacher. For this, the first assembly of the term, I don't go to sit with the choir. Everyone meets in the hall, exchanges up-to-date news, holiday gossip and sit cross-legged as our headmistress inspires us to great things.

Today Gill is with me. I haven't told the gang about her but we're all nice people and there isn't a problem. I introduce her. Now our gang numbers seven and for three years we stick together like glue.

Someone once said we have friends for different reasons and friends for different seasons. Gill and I live in Harpenden so see each other at weekends, Hazel and I are in the same maths group so chat on the phone when the homework is sticky. Xana and I are soulmates, in several subject sets together and share a wicked sense of humour. If there's fun to be had, Xana and I are in the thick of it.

This year our form tutor is an American who teaches history on an exchange year and while she can make it interesting, she's not a match for previous ones.

Third formers are either already fourteen, as are Gill and I, or rising fourteen and notoriously badly behaved. In girls' schools giggling can be profoundly debilitating. We giggle about anything mundane until our sides ache and the stricter the teacher and more embarrassing the situation the more we giggle. So this is how we start our third year.

Our American visitor is clearly unused to fourteen-year-old English girls. I have found my feet in the school and for now we see no reason to settle down to hard work. The fourth form is when O level work begins. Until then we want fun.

One day, the topic is Elizabeth the First and she asks the question, 'Why do you think Elizabeth did not marry or have children?'

There's a long pause after which I put up my hand.

'Yes?'

I feign innocence, my aim to raise a laugh.

'Perhaps she had no sex appeal?' Hoots of laughter erupt.

The teacher examines me disarmingly trying to hide the fact she knows the aim of my answer is to create disturbance. Her serious answer brings giggles. After this, we harness many more antics to liven up her lessons.

But we're not to get away with this for long. At the end of the first term the headmistress, Miss Dwyer, requests our form stay behind after assembly. She minces no words berating us for rudeness to a guest from America.

'You have given a very bad impression of English girls.'

Everyone looks down at the floor in embarrassment.

'I'm disappointed this has occurred in my school, of which I am so proud.'

Suddenly it dawns on me that I've been form captain for two terms in the second year and again for this first term in the third year. We hold a class meeting and decide I will go with my deputy form captain to give an apology to Miss Dwyer. At one point I am in tears that we have disgraced ourselves on my watch. I will never be form captain again, I think.

In term two we have a new history teacher. Our American is teaching keen first and second formers who behave impeccably. My fear about not being voted captain is unfounded. In the first tutorial my form votes me in for another term; a surprise after our disgrace. I've lived through the Christmas holidays dreading discovery jumping every time the phone rings. But no tell-tale phone call and no further recrimination.

Meanwhile we are still making mischief. Xana, Anna and I have a new chemistry teacher with a strange voice. Good mimicking practice but Xana is better than me.

Her enthusiasm for the subject isn't lost on us. We have experimental ideas of our own to make her experiments go wrong. One day we're taken into the school grounds to collect soil.

'Now the soil in the school grounds is alkali and not

acid so your litmus paper will not change colour when we test it.'

Wanna bet?

Xana and I collect our samples and return to the chemistry lab where we come up with the idea to add some hydrochloric acid from untouched jars on the science benches.

'Have you all got your samples?'

'Yes,' we answer in unison.

We hide our pot below the bench, sneaking the bottle of acid away from its position at the same time. We add the acid and queue to have our sample tested. All our classmates file back to their seats with the litmus paper colour unchanged.

I move forward and hand her our pot. There's a pause as she pushes the litmus paper in. A sudden drastic change of colour is an absolute delight.

'Oh,' she exclaims, 'what has happened?' We look appropriately interested and ask why this should be.

There's a long silence while the three of us stare silently at the litmus paper. For girls prone to bad attacks of the giggles, we are unbelievably straight faced.

'Oh,' she says, 'perhaps it's had a dog on it.'

The next week our chemistry teacher takes us all out to the Spinney. STAGGS boasts about three spinneys; two of these permanently out of bounds but one houses our den where the seven of us disappear at break and lunchtimes. Today we're in a front spinney with paper and pens. I stand behind Mrs A using her back subtly to support my note-taking.

'You use my back,' I say. In minutes the whole class is in line writing on each other's backs. When Mrs A turns, I lose my balance, and the whole line of girls collapses like a stack of dominoes.

These are the days of free school milk in one-third pint bottles and after first lesson we meet daily in the canteen. Later we meet outside the canteen to queue for school dinners. We feel privileged to be part of a gang of seven, all fans of Enid Blyton's *Secret Seven* and *Famous Five*, a secret not revealed at our interviews. Not for us lonely break times when a friend is absent.

October 1959

Just after my fourteenth birthday, my cousin visits and tells my mother about the local youth club. I am allowed to attend. As it's linked to our church Mum thinks all is decent.

St John's church hall is opposite the Rose and Crown public house. This hall, built in 1867 opposite the Plough and Harrow public house, was designed to meet the temporal and spiritual needs of the navvies working on the railway at the time. I hear trains from my bedroom window roaring along the same line we use to travel to London. The track crosses over Skew Bridge and Walkers Road Bridge. My mother says I can go to the youth club as long as I don't misbehave with the boys! As if I would?

Timothy is eighteen months older. Here I meet Margaret Ellis, whose father is the local chemist. Through her, I'm introduced to 45 rpm hit records and we practise our jiving and dancing to rock and roll records.

Other club members include the four children of the vicar, Mark Potts. Chris is the eldest son and I have a crush on him for two years. My mother knows the vicar's wife and belonged to her Young Wives' Club. Chris has two sisters, Hilary and Gilly, and a brother, Hugh.

My mother is prone to misinterpreting simple comments. One day the vicar's wife meets my mother in the street. She refers to the fact her four children find me fun. I am later cross questioned about this accolade. She can't believe fun is innocent. The games are innocuous, parlour-type games under the direction of a youth leader, whose great enthusiasm inspires young people. No game is inappropriate. We have debates and quizzes.

But now Mum is distracted by television's *Juke Box Jury* compered by David Jacobs with the signature tune of John Barry's 'Hit and Miss'. A panel of four guests sit and listen to single releases, then judge the hits (signalled at the end of the panels deliberations by a jolly ring) and the misses (hailed with a rasping hooter).

November 1959

Margaret Ellis and I are waiting outside the Plough and Harrow pub. It's not the first week we've done this. Invited to join others, waiting outside the pub is like wearing a badge of membership. An older boy brings us shandy. I'm nervous. I know I shouldn't be here. Margaret is unperturbed. There are fewer rules in her house.

The boy – perhaps my cousin – comes back with our drinks. Sipping shandy makes me feel more grown up than cups of tea in the hall kitchen.

Suddenly the door opens and a man appears. He stops and speaks to me.

It's my Uncle Frank. Oh no! He's Mum's cousin and bound to split on me. My heart sinks but I've been here before and my misdeeds weren't found out.

Unfortunately, this time they are.

The next afternoon after I come in from school my mother is quiet and then, when my father comes home from work, they say they know I've been standing drinking outside the Rose and Crown the night before. It's the road to ruin.

Finally, the biggest blow.

'We've decided you can't go to the youth club anymore.'

My mother watches my reaction and she cannot hide her pleasure at my discomfort especially as I had just made headway with a member of the opposite sex

The next day on the coach I tell Margaret. She's six months older than me but one year above me in school. She's now lost her youth club companion. I still see her in church on Sunday and afterwards we go to her home. They live above the chemist shop. She has a record player which is my idea of heaven. Her mother makes me welcome.

My luck changes after Mum meets our vicar's wife who expresses concern I'm not going to the club. The highlight of a Sunday for youth club members is to visit the vicarage after church. The family welcomes youth club youngsters and especially their children's friends. The vicarage boasts a playroom with a table tennis table and a record player complete with amplifier that plays 45 rpm records. These seven-inch records (known as singles), the first released in 1952. The *New Musical Express* sets up its hit parade to attract the new social group – *teenagers.*

I overhear that the vicar's wife suggested banning me from the youth club was not a good idea. Soon, my parents say I can go to the club again as long as I don't do the standing outside the pub thing. I return the next Sunday and gradually settle back into the dances, quizzes and general entertainment. Within a few weeks it's as if it never happened.

Meanwhile, Gill attends the youth club at St Nicholas Church just off Leyton Green. She also visits my youth club and her father collects her in his car. We don't have a car but my dad walks down Grove Avenue and waits in Grove Road for my return walk at 9.30pm. When a boy walks me home one Sunday, I see Dad hide in the shadows. I don't know who is more embarrassed, my dad or me.

I enjoy dancing. We jive to rock and roll by Bill Hailey and later learn the Twist. Girls dance together if boys don't ask them. The youth club leader teaches us different dances each week so we soon know The Veleta, the St Bernard Waltz, the Gay Gordons, The Cumberland Square Eight, Boston Two-Step and a Polka. Sometimes we finish with a Virginia Reel or the Sir Roger de Coverley and then the Last Waltz. Whoever asks you for this last dance is likely to ask you out or walk you home.

The fun dance is the Conga where we dance in a line with our hands on the hips of the person in front. The leader snakes about and takes the dancers outside into Southdown Road, sometimes into the kitchen and, worse, into the toilets and out again.

One week we learn the Limbo. Someone puts a stick across two chairs and we have to bend backwards and shuffle under it without touching it. We dance round to Chubby Checker's 'Limbo Rock'.

St Nicholas Youth Club meets on a Monday. One week our club is invited for a visit. Gill's father drives me home. That night I meet a boy from the boys' grammar school who asks me out. It's a special dance at St Nicholas Church Hall.

My parents oppose dates but I stand firm. When he arrives he's in full evening dress including a coat with a tail and a black bow tie. I am surprised but try to hide it. However, once at the hall, I soon realise the other boys are dressed in casual clothes and the only dances I enjoy are those where we change partners. I'm asked how I'm there with him. Not my idea of an enjoyable evening!

My parents' curiosity gets the better of them the next day and they ask if all the boys dressed up like that?

'Some were,' I mutter.

Summer 1959

Soon after I returned to the youth club my parents said that I could go on the school ski trip. To say I was happy was an understatement. Only the sporty girls would be going. Oh dear! I've never excelled at sport except netball but wondered if skiing could be different. Considering I could barely stay upright running on tarmac and frequently fell flat on my face on ice slides, I was bound to do worse at skiing.

For now I don't think about it. I know the ski trip will stretch the family coffers so, in the summer term, I visit the Red House (later the Harpenden Memorial Hospital). I knock and ask if there are jobs available in the holidays. I will do any job however menial. I'm shown into Matron's office. She's smart, forbidding and my legs tremble.

There's silence as she shuffles papers, tuts to herself, before looking up.

'You can work in the kitchen!'

Kitchen workers provide meals for in-patients and live-in staff such as nurses.

I will do split shifts. I have no idea what she means but soon learn this involves starting work at 7.30am and leaving at 1pm to return again at 4pm until 7.30pm. I'm therefore available for serving the breakfasts to nursing staff, laying tables, clearing away, washing up, chopping cabbage and peeling potatoes for the evening meal. Then I serve lunch to nursing staff and clear away. Afterwards it's washing up and a fast exit as I grab my bicycle to pedal home for two hours' break. I flop in a chair, sometimes with my library book, my legs and arms aching and my hands sore and chapped from chopping, cleaning and scrubbing. Soon it's time to pedal back. One perk is I don't go hungry. Once the staff have finished, the kitchen staff sit and eat in the kitchen.

No-one is more surprised than my parents to see me getting out of bed to the alarm clock at 6.30am, washing, grabbing breakfast and pedalling up Southdown Road. I'm not known for early rising. I'm a bad sleeper, taking an hour or two to go to sleep and then waking in a stupor seven hours later. I'm called repeatedly to get out of bed in term time but now I can roll out of bed and out of the house with time to spare. But I'm tired all the time and, after three weeks, exhausted. I line up every Thursday to get my wages. It's the most money I've had in my life and I clutch it tightly as I leave the building. It's been hard earned and every pay day I take the money to the post office and pay it into my savings account. I never touch a penny until the day before the ski trip.

January 1960

Before Christmas my mother attends a ski meeting, coming home armed with a list. She then takes me shopping for hideous items including long johns. She also knits overly large socks in oiled wool, recommended by the Bod. I travel with Xana and one of the Swedish twins, Eva Hallgren, to Champery in Switzerland. I am kitted out in bulky ski pants also recommended by the Bod. By the time I arrive at Victoria I can only waddle like a lame penguin. I complain my ski pants are too big but they came from a catalogue.

'Never mind,' says Mum. 'At least we've got Green Shield stamps.'

On the Channel Ferry I spend most of the crossing in the toilets, which, in the rough and turbulent January seas, are occupied by several other seasick travellers. On the overnight train matters do not improve. It's a budget ski trip and eight of us must sleep bolt upright in the standard compartment. As slumber often follows travel sickness, I fall into a deep sleep, waking later to find three of my fellow travellers curled up on the floor while I am stretched out over the whole seat. Luckily, they have sympathy for my plight.

Neither do I distinguish myself at the sport. After all, I can't stay upright on dry land so there's no hope on snow and ice. Fortunately, a fellow beginner is worse than me which distracts the instructor. She gets the name 'The One Who Got Away'. It also makes my frequent downward crashes with skis criss-crossed in the air less noticeable. How I hate those ski lessons. I spend all week trying to stay upright. The weight of all my ski clothes renders my rise to a vertical position impossible, often requiring help from my ski mates.

The ski lift is a pole with a small round seat. On the first occasion I miss the seat and am transported up the slope with my bottom trailing two inches from the snow, my feet dangling over the pole. I hang on for dear life until the lift passes a connecting pole when a jolt sends me flying off. My skis then begin a slow backwards descent only halted by the shouts of the next skier who is facing a collision with my backside. To avoid disaster, I throw myself to the side of the track and roly-poly several yards. Here my vast padding is put to good use.

After several attempts to right myself I'm pulled to a vertical position by a *REAL SKIER* (a handsome one who arrives in a flurry of snow performing the perfect stop). I make a note to repeat this accident the next day and get repeat attention from this fit guy. Meanwhile, I trudge sideways up the slope so I can ski down again, not that you could call what I do skiing. After five days of this palaver I doubt I will ever recover. My body is one large bruise and every muscle aches. On day five's assessment I'm in the bottom group.

Xana and Eva Hallgren are put in an advanced skiing

class – they've been skiing before – so I don't see much of them during the day. I doubt I'll even get an attendance certificate. However, I pass the bronze test. On my return home, I play down my hopeless skiing ability and absent sense of balance so my parents don't feel they've wasted money. They are impressed with my bronze badge!

Another trip that year is an outing to Derbyshire's Peak District. I often envy my sister's disappearances back to boarding school so I am excited about a week away and jubilant at the thought of staying at a Youth Hostel. Not so. Once away from home and its comforts, I discover it's not the fun I anticipated. The weather is wet, the hostel cold, the food colourless and I am homesick. Packed lunch is dry bread and tasteless meat I can't identify. Neither can I escape more travel sickness. Other than one very long walk to church, the week is full of coach journeys. I am required to travel in the front missing all the fun.

As third formers we are not averse to mischief and experimentation. On our trip to Malham, Xana and I plan to sample tobacco. We wait until our dormitory mates are asleep before raising ourselves from beneath the covers, creeping out of bed, tiptoeing barefoot across the cold linoleum floor to the toilets. Once there, huddled in a cubicle, we light up, cough and splutter, but bask in the euphoria that follows such a brazen adventure.

One evening Gill follows us and enters a nearby cubicle. Xana and I hold our breaths and try not to take a drag for fear of being found out. But our sense of cunning is cut short when we hear her say our names! 'Are you cooking bacon in there?' Xana and I laugh about this for years afterwards. 'No,' we say, 'we'll be back in a minute.'

After a week of lost sleep and little pleasure – neither of us enjoy our puffs – we are mortified to discover other pupils smoking openly in their dorms. Fourteen-year-olds lounge nonchalantly on their beds, dragging on cigarettes, blatantly puffing up eddies of smoke.

I often wonder if it was worth all the discomfort and loss of sleep, as my mother smells smoke on my clothes and, having recently resumed the habit herself, on lighting up her own cigarette one evening, she holds out the packet to me.

'I know you do!' She says with a glint in her eye.

That puts me firmly in my place.

May 1960

The highlight of 1960 is the opening of the open-air swimming pool in Rothamsted Park on 7th May. Gill and I see this pool as a place to meet the opposite sex.

We shop in Luton as we need some fashion. We spend our meagre allowance in Dolcis on shoes almost impossible to wear. Hobbling springs to mind. But at last I have shoes similar to those the girls bring for Dad to repair. Stilettos! I have no fears they might end up beyond repair. He is so clever with his hands. We return clutching large carrier bags of fashionable outfits, wide belts to cinch our dresses at the waist, and low-cut swimsuits for the swimming pool. My mother isn't impressed.

'It'll have to go back,' she says in despair. 'There's no way you can wear that.'

'Why?'

'You'll be having the boys swarming around you and you'll get up to no good.'

I put the shopping away and keep quiet while Mum she soon forgets about taking my purchases back to the shop.

However, the discovery at fifteen that an attractive swimsuit can draw admirers is all I need for swimming to suddenly become popular. Gill and I go to Rothamsted Park in all weathers and lie down posed on our towels. If we venture into the pool our heads stay well out of the water so that our newly rollered and backcombed hair doesn't turn into frizzy rats' tails while unforeseen splashes could cause our cheap mascara to dribble black marks.

Meanwhile, word has got around and the boys at St John's Youth Club saunter through Rothamsted Park and sidle up to the fence which skirts the swimming pool. There's grass round the sides, great for sunbathing. Gill and I enjoy an occasional flirt at the fence with rarely anyone to tell on us.

I never tell my parents of the incident at the swimming pool. Gill and I always go as soon as it opens in the spring. We splash about reminding ourselves of breast stroke, crawl and other strokes enjoying being back in the water. There are no indoor swimming pools at that time. Venturing to the deep end, something that was never a problem before, now causes me difficulty. Suddenly, I feel tired all over, my legs drag me downwards and I sink unable to keep myself afloat on the surface. I come up for air twice when I feel a strong arm around me pulling me out. I find myself in the recovery position on the edge of the pool choking and spitting water. Gill says I was about to drown and a boy pulled me out. The lifeguard reminds us that on your first swim of the year you should take it easy.

My parents never told me that.
And I never told them I'd nearly drowned.

September 1960

As much as I'd like to share hilarious moments of my school day, I censor my tales. Despite my love of singing and music, any non-academic lesson warrants some mischief making from my friends and me. In the first and second form music lessons are taken by Miss Macey who stands no nonsense. But this is to change.

In the third form, a new music teacher arrives, a young attractive woman, heavily made up, wearing fashionable full skirts, 1950s style, and teetering on the highest of stiletto heels. In September she couldn't be missed tripping through the entrance hall, her heels disobeying the rules of silence. These stilettos are the highest my classmates have seen. Of course, I see them in Dad's shop.

This young teacher trains us with the song of the day and then says, 'Stand'. She perches on a chair, precariously poised in her five-inch high heels, her skirt billowing at eye level, conducting enthusiastically with a baton. We all suffer giggles and are sent out frequently. On one occasion, I hide behind a bookcase on the landing as Miss Macey heads up the stairs. Too late, I'm caught and lectured.

Meanwhile, the opposite sex becomes more attractive by the day. My only chance to meet boys is the church youth club. Others are luckier. Around 1960 a café, La Capri, opens up on Leyton Green. Adjacent to the *Harpenden Free Press* newspaper office, the rooms have tables, chairs and there is frothy coffee we've never seen before. We don't know it then but it is the start of American mass culture.

My mother thinks it is full of Teddy boys and I'm forbidden to go. Inside beyond an arch through strips of plastic, which serve as a curtain, there's a dimmed area where teenagers smooch and listen to music from something called a jukebox.

Around this time, milk bars start to appear in northern towns. Their customers are boys aged fifteen to twenty with drape suits. Also, an entrepreneur Charles Forte opens one in Upper Regent Street. Forte's answer to post-war gloom is to paint these in red and white stripes with his counter girls dressed in red and white costumes. But the jukebox, an evolution of the American nickelodeon, encourages the adolescents inside. I desperately want to frequent La Capri and play the jukebox. I know girls who go but never challenge my parents.

However, Mum doesn't stunt my performing ability completely. When I put on concerts at Christmas or Easter, she's a willing participant, although, prior to the event, I'm quizzed about the script to reduce her embarrassment.

1960 – The Russians are Coming...

'I blame it on the Russians!' My grandmother's proclamation raises, once again, the question of the Cold War. Mum tries to explain but until I obtain a CND badge at fourteen, the hostile relationship between Russia and America is of little interest.

My grandmother blames everything on the Russians.

'They must have let off another bomb,' she says as the rain pours down.

In fact, in Granny's book, the Russians are responsible for everything wrong in Britain.

However, on Sundays there is one topic of conversation. A never-ending tale of sawdust on Granny's garden path plus blood, gristle and raw meat trickles by her back door. The butcher's next door to Dad's shop employs noisy Saturday boys who clean boards and knives on Granny's path leaving Granny's garden transformed into a swirling mess of red water and sawdust. Walking through animal parts just isn't her style.

However, Granny is a great joiner; a Women's Institute member, her picture frequently in the local paper. She sings in the WI choir every Friday. They enter concerts and competitions regularly winning the regional cup. In her younger days, she joined the Salvation Army, despite being Church of England. My mother refuses to talk about this affiliation insisting the Sally Ann provided an outlet for her singing rather than religion. Saturday nights saw her in public houses encouraging drinkers to repent.

Every May, once we have the television, Cup Final day sees her in our sitting room at 1.30, singing 'Abide with Me' and all the other hymns. Her wonderful singing voice and love of music is also present in my mother, who attends church singing in a strident voice.

While we joked about my grandmother and her constant doom and gloom speeches about the Russians and the atomic bomb, the 1960s were a time of anxiety and the Cold War showed no sign of ending.

1956-1957 – Play and Perform

I'm not allowed to play on the street. While I made dens and used a tent on the lawn, others played out in the lanes and nearby roads, often riding their bicycles up and down past my house or gathering into groups in the spinneys, setting up camps in trees and bushes. Mum doesn't like the boys who wear drainpipe trousers and winkle picker shoes, rock 'n' roll or jive. The only news to cheer her is Harold Macmillan telling us 'we have never had it so good'. We now have a fridge, a hairdryer and two electric fires. Last week Dad asked Uncle Frank, an electrician, to put a wall electric fire in the bathroom.

This restriction on playing in spinneys or in the street didn't prevent my social popularity. Linda, Douglas and Elsa regularly call for me. Sometimes I preferred to play alone.

'She's just in a dream world!' Mum often complains to my father. 'She doesn't help and she's in another world!'

'Never mind.' Dad sticks up for me. 'She'll grow out of it.'

But I don't grow out of writing. I suggest I do journalism but am told I'm not tough enough. You have to be 'hard' to work on a paper.

And then,

'Writing won't get your bread and butter.'

I'm not sure what she means.

'You need a proper job and career.'

As well as discouraging my writing, I run into other difficulties. One activity is baking but I make a mess and use too many eggs.

However, television is a main feature in sitting rooms and living rooms and I start to take more interest. Comedic characters such as Norman Wisdom and Mr Pastry brought laughter and slapstick was enjoyed by my sister as well.

I love programmes with horses such as *Champion the Wonder Horse* and *The Lone Ranger* calling out 'Hi-Ho Silver' plus his companion, Tonto, who calls him Kemosabe. Later there's *Wagon Train* and *The Saturday Night Variety Show* but my favourite is *Sunday Night at the London Palladium* and, surprisingly, I am allowed to stay up.

Before long I'm watching more adult programmes. *What's My Line?* chaired by Eamonn Andrews, where a panel including Barbara Kelly and Lady Isabel Barnet have to guess the person's job from a mime.

We watch *This is Your Life* (also with Eamonn Andrews). Mum's a fervent admirer of Perry Como who sings 'Magic Moments' while sitting in a rocking chair wearing hand-knitted sweaters which Mum believes were lovingly made by his wife.

'Such a nice man.' Mind you, she called Harold Wilson the same. As my parents met at ballroom dancing classes, they're fans of *Come Dancing* with Victor Sylvester but that's too late in the evening for me.

Saturday nights, a roaring fire and fans of *Dixon of Dock Green* are gripped with crime stories. I daydream of working with Andy, PC Dixon's son-in-law. As well as my writing, I fancy myself as a television actress although I've little idea how I'll realise my ambition. The whole family watch *Juke Box Jury* (1959) and discuss whether the song will be a hit or a miss – of course, only when my sister's away. When she's home we both watch programmes like *Danger Man* (1960), *Dr Kildare*, *Dr Finlay's Casebook* and *The Fugitive* (1962). We take turns to tell her what's happening on screen. Subtitles are yet to come.

Around 1958 I watch the *Billy Cotton Band Show*. This is broadcast live on a Saturday night. I love to see my pianist hero, Russ Conway, perform. I play 'Side Saddle' over and over in my head and soon head for the Luton music shop and come home with the sheet music. Sometimes, my piano teacher will search for a piece of music I'll like. Then I sit painstakingly practising the tune until I'm note-perfect. Russ's later hit, 'Roulette', is also featured on the show and, again, I venture to get the sheet music. By now, I'm a Russ Conway fan, although people think this tame, preferring to idolise Bob Haley playing 'Rock Around the Clock' or Elvis Presley. But I'm also an Elvis fan and Gill and I take ourselves off to watch Elvis films such as *Jailhouse Rock*, *Blue Hawaii* and *Love me Tender*.

Russ Conway, born Trevor Herbert Stanford, was in the charts in 1959 for eighty-three weeks. Two of the instrumentals, 'Side Saddle' and 'Roulette' are self-penned, the latter deposes his hit 'A Fool Such as I'.

Pop music is the fashion. As well as *Juke Box Jury,* Pete Murray has singers and groups on his *Six-Five Special.*

However, the crème de la crème on television has to be the advent of the Beatles – four clean-looking, fresh-faced, guitar-playing lads from Liverpool. This hysteria is known as Beatlemania. When they appear on television, we swoon as they strum and sing.

Pets and People

I'd love a dog but Mum says she'd have to walk it and there's not enough money to feed an animal.

'You've got other pets.'

At the bottom of Grove Avenue a neighbour has a pet corgi that sits on the path outside the house and never wanders.

'You're always sitting down the road with that dog.'

I don't answer.

'Just be careful. Not every dog is nice.'

That summer, visiting my cousin in Rickmansworth and bored with adult conversation, I venture out, and see a dog tied up. I move forward to pat it but it leaps at me growling. Too late I run. The Alsatian lands on my fast-retreating calf sinking teeth into my flesh. Hearing my screams, everyone comes running. I'm cleaned up, my mother saying I should have known better. I think I'll avoid dogs for a while.

My sister's tortoise is a surrogate pet in term time. School finishes, a twenty-minute bus ride and I find my mother sitting in the garden with a tray of tea, bread, butter, jam and cakes. Daisy's wire run is on the back lawn. She hears the gate click and strides out of her little house to march round her wire pen, with head and neck fully stretched. Sometimes she even comes out before I reach the front gate. Mum says she's sure Daisy is telepathic and hears me coming up the road.

With Susan away, it's left to Mum and me to feed Daisy lettuce and dandelion flowers. Daisy loves dandelion flowers better than leaves and she eats several lettuces on hot June and July days. Dad sets rows of lettuces, staggering the seeding and planting to ensure a constant supply of young juicy plants. Luckily, she enjoys munching her way through the bolted lettuces, chomping through the thick stem.

My most controversial pet was a mouse. I'm amazed my parents agreed. My friend, Sally, from Welwyn Garden City, had pet mice, which reproduced regularly. When her mouse had babies I asked Mum if I could have one. My parents were amenable to my pets so no problem there. Sally brought the mouse to school in a shoe box and it sat on my desk all day moving from class to class with me. Eventually, I got him home in one piece on the bus. He lived in a cage in the garage. My sister, now living at home, complained about the smell which defied all my attempts to get rid of it.

In my teens I became a member of the PDSA, The People's Dispensary for Sick Animals. I held a small sale outside my front garden gate to raise money and sent them the proceeds. My mother arranged for a small paragraph to be written in the local paper about my endeavour. The junior section, the Busy Bees, sent a magazine which I read avidly. I also had a badge which I added to my CND one.

The Public Hall was a favourite place. It was where I

saw Gilbert and Sullivan operettas. On Saturdays before Christmas, I'd cycle to the Village, leave my bicycle at my dad's shop and go to the bazaars with my hard-earned money. Dances were held there on a Saturday night and my grandmother worked there as a cloakroom attendant, which gave her some spare cash. I wasn't allowed to go to those dances after my grandmother related tales of drunken girls.

A popular 1950s craze was the hula hoop. This was the first time a toy had become popular with most youngsters owning one. Competitions and demonstrations took off for young and old alike, and mass production ensured it was widely available. The manufacturers, Wham-O, sold 25,000,000 in the first two months alone. The craze crossed the Atlantic and few British homes were without one. Records for the most, fastest and longest spinning of the hoop are still set, but, for most people, the hula hoop remains a bit of fun. Once the craze lost its spiciness, hoops were used in stiff underskirts or petticoats, made with several layers of net sewn into the hem. This allowed the full material of the patterned skirt to be held out away from the legs, very fashionable in the late 1950s.

If hoops were not available we had other means of getting our skirts to stand out so they flew up in the jive. We used sugar and hot water to make starch and steeped the net before we hung them to dry. It's impossible to hang the skirt in the wardrobe as it takes up so much space and refuses to be squashed inside.

The problem with the hula hoop becomes evident at dances as on sitting down, if we sit on the back of the hula hoop ring, it flicks up in the air showing our knickers.

There is an art to sitting down in a hula hoop skirt and that is to hold the hoop up as you sit down so you sit in the hole. For this we need more room on the seats around the church hall where we sit waiting for a dance. Also when dancing with a boy this contraption in your skirt means he can't get too close. Probably for the best my mother would say. Anyway, the hula hoop craze didn't last long and my hoop was eventually consigned to the garage along with other crazes.

My friendship with Gill blossomed through our days at grammar school and we regularly visited each other's houses for tea. We loved weekly long walks and cycle rides when we had many laughs. I loved visiting her home. Gill told her parents I did a good impression of Cliff Richard singing 'Livin' Doll' so I sang to them which sent them into gales of laughter. After that it became my party piece and I would be asked to sing the song at school, parties and whenever our gang of seven met up. 'Living Doll' was in the charts for twenty-three weeks in 1959 and spent six weeks at number one. It was issued on 31st July 1959. 'Travelling Light', another of Cliff Richard's hits, spent five weeks at number one in the October of that year. 'Please Don't Tease Me' was Cliff's hit in the following year. I never told my parents how much Gill's family enjoyed my rendition of 'Livin' Doll'.

At weekends Gill and I take off on our bicycles. Sometimes her parents give us a map and ideas of where to go. We promise to stay together. Once we take a short cut across a field only to be chased by a bull escaping at speed and scraping ourselves under the fence just in time. We frequently get lost. Many times, we have to find a Village shop to ask the way. It amused us that Gill's parents said keep off the main roads and my parents said keep off the country lanes.

Harpenden boasts two cinemas. The Regent in Leyton Road has Saturday cinema. Gill and I prefer the Embassy on the Luton Road. We munch Smith's crisps hunting the salt in a blue waxed paper. Popcorn had not yet arrived in cinema kiosks but the usherette, who led us to our seats with a torch, came into the auditorium at the interval (usually after the supporting film and the Pathé News) with ice cream on a tray secured by a strap wound around her neck.

My hunger for books was partly satisfied via Harpenden Library in Vaughan Road. I'm introduced to the *Scarlet Pimpernel* books probably by Xana. These books, by Baroness Orczy, are a craze and I model my own writing on life in the French Revolution. My main character was Adeline, a French Countess, who helped victims escape the guillotine. Baroness Orczy's hero, Sir Percy Blakeney, is an English aristocrat at the Royal Court. It was possible to read the first two books before detecting his other second identity of being the Scarlet Pimpernel. The hero whisked French aristocrats away from under the noses of the revolutionaries so they weren't sent to the guillotine. He's named Scarlet Pimpernel because he left drawings of the flower at the scene. However, the crème de la crème of our reading was *Exodus* by Leon Uris. Despite its huge size, it's passed around. We'd all watched a plethora of war films which featured the capture and incarceration of the

Jews. *The Diary of Anne Frank* was an emotional hit on the book circuit.

Interestingly, while I rarely see my parents reading books, they do read two papers each day, the *Daily Express* and the *Evening News*. TV news is limited and our television is in the hardly-used sitting room.

But I have a hunger for words, devouring everything in print at home. Our bookcase with glass doors displays a full set of Dickens hardbacks. Poetry was a great love, my source of rhyme and poetry via Arthur Mee encyclopaedias.

Meanwhile, Gill and I continue to frequent the cinema, seeing Cliff Richard films and films about the Second World War. I see *Dunkirk* with my mother, who describes it as harrowing although I see it as a great achievement.

'You're too young to understand,' she says.

'So many troops snatched from the beaches before the Germans arrived.'

My parents always stood for the national anthem at the end of a film or show and I continued this with Gill. We both wait while others make for the exits.

Another film I saw with Mum was Kenneth More in *Genevieve*, where a veteran car owner attempts the London to Brighton Run. I loved the film and music but particularly the trumpet solo of Kay Kendall although I was to find out that someone else played it. Kenneth More was a heartthrob and I desperately willed him to win what was a race between him and John Gregson. It's testament to Kenneth More's fame that an article appeared in my 1958 *Girl Annual* relating his life and acting successes.

Somehow, this might be tame for thirteen-year-olds today.

In 1958, Mum and I see Kenneth More in *A Night to Remember*, the story of *Titanic*, a ship said to be unsinkable, but which sank after hitting an iceberg on its first night at sea in the Atlantic.

A year later we see the film, *A Summer Place*, based on *Peyton Place*. It was released with beautiful theme music by Percy Faith Orchestra. I wanted to play that on the piano.

And Into Work

Once back at school in September 1959, I find school friends have Saturday and holiday jobs, earning serious money. The talk is of Alfred Marks, Brook Street and Reed agencies. After a typing test, they send you where they want. Dad has the *Evening News* but says the *Evening Standard* is best if you are looking for a job.

One friend works in W H Smith. I love books and writing so I envy her. After all, a discounted shorthand notebook wouldn't go amiss. She received the glorious sum of £1 for her Saturday work. Another friend worked in Woolworth's, for many years a penny store opened in 1879. They enjoyed perks including cheaper sweets bought by the quarter pound in paper bags and, every Friday night, her dad gave her a list of screws and nails to buy for his weekend jobs.

Probably my first unpaid job was weeding and stoning our garden for Dad. I loved doing it but the accolade from my father and the happy look on his face was enough. The hospital kitchen work was my second job and I was paid for it. But my next paid work was a big surprise. I wasn't looking for it, I didn't apply for it nor was I interviewed.

At fourteen years of age I need cash for fashionable

clothing to wear at the local youth club, money for make-up to daub on my face to hide the start of dreaded acne. My sister suffered spots but so far I'd been spared. So, I take a deep breath and suggest to my parents I get a Saturday job. My words are met with silence. For my mother getting a job in those two shops was definitely 'out'. My father, on the other hand, was less judgemental, patting me on the head and saying not to rush into anything.

'I have ideas.'

'Don't go getting a job just yet.'

'Why?'

'I might be able to come up with something.'

And he did. Two days later he raised the subject at dinner.

'Would you like to work a Saturday morning for me?'

'Only the morning?'

I thought of the measly ten shillings – half of the wages my friends earned.

'Yes, but I'll give you fifteen shillings.'

Wow! The maths was easy. That was a good deal. I didn't have to work a whole day for one pound. I could work the morning and, after lunch, would go to St Albans and spend my earnings. I had work *and* freedom. After all, fifteen shillings would buy a pair of shoes.

My dad's mouth twitches with pleasure. Mum says he offered me the job so he could see more of me. It occurred to me that when I have my own money, I can buy what I like.

The next Saturday saw me up early and cycling towards the Village.

This was the main centre of Harpenden but it's

certainly not a village in the late 1950s since city workers began to find it an attractive forty-minute commute to St Pancras. Houses are springing up everywhere so my home village is beginning to resemble a town.

Rather unfit since starting an academic grammar school with two hours' homework each night and little opportunity for sport, I huffed and puffed all the way. Gym and games were certainly not my forte. I'd do anything to avoid prancing up to the horse in the gym to do a leap. It was more a grapple for me and I often fell backwards.

I was, in today's language, a 'wimp'.

So how was I to survive working in Dad's shoe repair shop?

It was easier than I thought. I loved serving customers, taking their money and going to the wooden till in the workroom. I take pride in giving the correct amount of change. Thanks to good maths teaching I never make a mistake.

'Count it out into their hand.' Dad is training me.

I bag up the finished shoes and write the name on the bag. They're put on the shelves in alphabetical order. I cut up tickets from cardboard, punch holes and then tie the ticket to the laces, if there are any. I take in shoes for repair and, if in doubt, I take them and ask Dad.

On a Saturday, customers include young girls with stilettos worn down or even broken. Dad buys a special drill so he can repair the stiletto heels. He gets the most stubborn screw out of the heel.

The girls are delighted but sometimes the damage is so great they have to be sent away for new heels. Girls at work are willing to pay 15/- (fifteen shillings) for new heels on their favourite shoes.

The weeks pass and my confidence grows; shop work is in the blood. My mother worked in a department store from the age of twelve and then managed Granddad's shop after his stroke. These days she works afternoons in Dad's shop and often stands in for other assistants if they are ill, sometimes at short notice. Dad phones when someone fails to arrive and Mum duly mounts her bicycle and pedals furiously to get there come rain or shine. She loved dealing with customers.

I learn about Dad's trade during these years behind the counter. The shop, C Smith Shoe Repairs, is at the bottom of Station Road. Customers think my dad's surname is Smith and few are aware Mum is married to my dad who is quite handsome.

Women then flirt with my dad which Mum finds amusing. They make it clear they do not want to be served by a fourteen-year-old girl.

'Can I speak to Mr Smith?' This always raises a laugh in the workshop.

When there are no customers I watch Dad and his workman, young Ken, hone their craft. I wear nylon overall as the smell of leather, dust and fixative penetrated our clothes and hair. I always showered and washed my hair as soon as I arrived home.

All the shelves in the workroom and the shop were built by Dad. The shelves are labelled with the day of the week and, once a shelf is full, it's necessary to promise collection for the following day. Usually by midday on Saturday I have filled the Tuesday and Wednesday shelves so from then on I am promising for Thursday.

There's good reason the shop is packed with work. Only the very best craftsmen are employed and the shop has an excellent reputation for a high standard of work. Some shoes are brought in so that previous shoddy workmanship carried out elsewhere can be put right. Some try to say they have been repaired at Smith's but Dad knows his stock so he doesn't stand any nonsense.

The first job when repairing the shoes was to use strong pliers to strip the existing sole and heel with the shoe placed upside down on a last. Then the appropriate materials were matched in size to the shoe. All the materials are in boxes labelled with the heel size with the workman selecting the appropriate size and material. Some heels were rubber and some people asked for leather. Leather came in a large sheet and my father traces round the heel and then cuts it out. The shoe surfaces are roughed up with a wire brush in preparation for gluing. This glue, a special fixative purchased from Dad's supplier, was left for a while and the sole or heel was similarly glued and left. When surfaces are ready they're fixed together and another hand tool is used to press surfaces together firmly. Dad would have several pairs waiting with glue at a time. Then the edges were cut flush with a sharp knife. My heart would leap at this point as some of the ladies' shoes were very delicate but no harm came to them. Dad had all shoe colours in Meltonian cream jars and the newer brand of Tuxan became popular making scuffs invisible. Sometimes the new sole had to be stitched to the shoe.

Dad also works on other items such as bags and sandal

straps. There was a small heavy duty sewing machine for this.

I'm curious about why my father offered me the job but all was eventually revealed.

His eyes twinkle and he leans forward to whisper.

'No daughter of mine will clean toilets.'

Yes, he'd asked around the Village to find out what was expected of Saturday girls.

'Make the boss a coffee and take it to his office.' Hmm.

Clean the toilets after the manager had returned from the pub and graced it with the output of his lunch. Hmm.

No, my father saved me from this and probably worse.

I'm forever grateful and loved working with him seeing his look of pride as I dance my way to the till singing a Beatles song.

1960-1961 – Forbidden Books, Clothes and Pirate Radio

'Have you got it?' I have my school satchel and some paper inside waiting. Xana hands me a book covered in brown paper. I can't wait to get my hands on it.

'Well?' I ask. 'Is it really dirty?'

'Yes, in places.'

'Good.'

'You'll like it.'

I take the book and stuff it in the deepest depths of my leather satchel. Now the big problem lurches up to stop me in my tracks. How am I going to read this book without my mother finding out? I wrap it in the spare paper and put schoolbooks on top of it. Perhaps I can find time in the lunch break to start reading.

'What have you got there?' Gill has seen us huddled together.

Anna and Sally arrive at the canteen. We're in our usual places near the server drinking our free milk. Both girls take bottles, press the straw into the top and start drinking. Judy and Hazel are next. Now we're all drinking the milk except the book is burning a hole in the bottom of my satchel. How long will I be able to leave it there, I am not sure.

'It's so hot.' Gill is fanning herself with an exercise book.

'Shall we go to our sunbathing place at lunchtime?'

'Yes.' I think our special place is private enough.

'Have you got your special lotion?' Judy looks hot. Gill nods and grins. She has concocted a lotion of lemon juice and olive oil plus some other ingredients which all combined ensure your flesh fries in the sun. I can't wait to get that on either.

We were nearly caught one week at the back of the school buildings. There we were with our blouse tops undone and spread-eagled in the sun when a prefect comes round the corner of Breakspear block.

'What are you doing?' It's a warning she's approaching. Many a prefect would've known better and approached silently to catch fourth formers in their misdemeanours. Last week, hearing her, we tucked our blouses in quickly and hid our bras in our bags. By the time she reached us we all looked sombrely dressed with French books set out for revision.

'I'll be watching you lot.' We note to be more alert. Next time we might not be so lucky.

Today we eat lunch quickly and disappear in twos and threes into the maze of walkways around the grammar school site. When we reach the back of Breakspear block, Gill is already half-dressed and covered in her sun lotion. One by one we lie down, our tops exposed, some of us sunning our backs while we read our latest book, Mary Wakefield. Judy started this craze as her older sister had read the Mazo de la Roche books. Once I discovered these, Harpenden Library had never seen me so often as that summer.

I look over towards Gill. Her face and front of her chest outside her brassiere are slowly going red and her face bright scarlet. She's blonde with fair skin and she's frying herself. I've lifted my skirt to expose my legs and rub in some lotion. Ten minutes later my legs are stinging with burn.

'Whatever have you put in this?'

When I look I see Anna is bright red too. Anna is a redhead and she shouldn't be sunbathing. She's like my auburn-haired mother who has to cover up when we're at the seaside. Our blue and white uniform two pieces are sprinkled around on the grass. We are unlikely to get away with it if we are caught. In the distance the bell rings for the start of afternoon lessons. We make for our lockers and grab the necessary books. I stuff the French books on top of the brown paper lump in my satchel. I might have a chance next lesson, I think, to have a quick read.

But I don't get the chance until I get home.

'I am going to do my homework.' My mother nods and I disappear with my satchel into the sitting room. There I sit flicking through the pages looking for a rude word or phrase. The chapters aren't named so there's no guidance as to when some ripe language might appear. I know Lady Chatterley is meeting the gamekeeper but of course, everyone knows that. The publishers have been in court and the book has been banned. How Xana got a copy I'll never know. It's not available in Harpenden Library. Lady Chatterley's Lover by D H Lawrence was renowned in 1961 for being banned under the Obscenity Act, but not before several copies had been sold and passed around. Someone (again probably Xana) obtained a copy and she covered it in brown paper and concealed it further inside a thick brown envelope. It was passed around our form group but only to those we trusted. The book, published in 1928, was always in someone's satchel, hidden amongst homework. While titillating and explicit, it was less obscene than the litigation news coverage suggested. In fact, a thin storyline, unbelievable characters, despite social and political commentary, meant we found it less riveting than expected.

'I do have another book you'll like.' *Peyton Place* by Grace Metalious caused uproar in America because the townspeople recognised themselves. On 6 December 1957, the original Dell edition of Peyton Place was placed on the banned list, remaining there until 11 February 1971. It was the book's sexual passages, rather than its handling of taboo subjects, that concerned the censors.

'Yes, bring it in.' I am up for anything.

In fact, anything I read provides my own ideas for my next novel – not that my writing is long enough to be a novel but I'm plodding on. I always have an audience. Most of our form wants to be the first to hear the story of my next book or the next chapter contents. Narrating the story in the back row of the French class stimulates me and stimulates more ideas. It's annoying if we are asked a question by the French teacher. It's a wonder I pass French but I get a grade 3 – surprising when you consider my inattention.

At the moment I am writing about Adeline. The name comes from the Whiteoak family whose matriarch and grandmother is called Adeline. She never liked Mary Wakefield even when her son married her. I spend the evening skimming pages, looking for the sex bits as Xana calls them. The next day I say I haven't found anything yet.

'It's two thirds of the way through.' That's when Lady Chatterley meets the gamekeeper.

When I do find it on the second night I don't understand the words. Xana enlightens me. Apparently, the f- word means having sex. It's new to me.

I now have to pass the brown paper covered book to Hazel who finds it equally puzzling but our quest for the pornographic – another word we don't understand and cannot ask about – is interrupted by the announcement Miss Dwyer makes in assembly.

'Girls, for the school's birthday on 17th May we will have a service in the Abbey starting at 10 o'clock and in the afternoon we will have games in the hall.'

'What, all of us?' Seven hundred girls? Apparently some will do activities outside.

The most important part of the announcement is a talent competition. Xana and I decide to do a rendition of the Everly Brothers singing 'Walk Right Back'. We rehearse every break and lunchtime until we've perfected it. On the day, the prize goes to someone who plays a piece of Beethoven on the piano and we are sorely disappointed.

Later, I am sitting in my bedroom listening to the *Top Twenty* with Alan Freeman on radio. I have to listen until the end when he reads the whole top twenty, even naming those in the top thirty or forty. There are adverts for Horace Batchelor's method of winning money on the football pools.

Now my favourite singers are Pat Boone and the Everly Brothers. I sing along with songs such as '*Born too Late*' and '*Volare*'.

The pirate station radio Luxembourg is a favourite but in 1964 it meets competition from Radio Caroline whose disc jockeys play pop music. Getting a good signal is a struggle at times, but I fiddle with the tuning buttons. Radio Caroline is one of the first pirate radio ships broadcasting pop music from the North Sea. The disc jockeys are ferried to and fro and sometimes experience a mill pond and other times a Force 10 gale. They broadcast twenty-four-hour music from a boat just off Sheerness. A film at that time, *The Boat that Rocked*, is based on the lives of disc jockeys (DJs) on Radio Caroline. In rough weather, the DJs had to put a half crown coin (2 shillings and 6 pence) on top of the stylus so it would not jolt. I listened to Radio Caroline and Radio Luxembourg on the large cabinet radio on my dressing table. One of the pirate DJs was Tony Blackburn. Tony Benn, MP, in an interview, said he hated it and wanted enforcement action.

However, now I listen to pop music on television. *Jukebox Jury,* chaired by David Jacobs, was a weekly panel show that gave new releases marks out of five. Each week he played a selection of 7" singles on a large juke box to a panel of four celebrities. Janice Nicholls, a teenager, also gave her verdict with 'Oi'll give it foive' on '*Thank Your Lucky Stars*' hosted by Brian Matthew.

But, I haven't abandoned the *Light Programme* completely as I tune in to *The Navy Lark* with Leslie

Phillips who directs the ship by guesswork with laughs from Jon Pertwee. *Take it from Here* and *The Goons* also provide much enjoyment.

* * *

My mother's fashions change in the fifties. Now, she wears full-skirted dresses, often from Horrockses, sometimes called shirtwaisters if the top half has buttons and collar and the lower half has a full skirt. But in the late fifties the fashion for trousers or slacks found her wearing trousers rather than skirts. However, femininity was the keyword in the fifties and women like my mother preferred skirts. Jeans were only recently available for younger women. Mum wouldn't have worn jeans. No way.

1961 – We Are Car Owners!

For fifteen years I've walked, cycled or used the 321 bus. But this new acquisition changes that. After watching neighbours drive for years, we join the club. Somewhere in the deep recesses of his bank account Dad finds spare cash for a Morris Minor. He parks it on the front garden mixing cement to extend the path. He surveys it with pride and we stand around making approving noises. Lessons are planned. By 1961 the Morris Minor 1000 is so popular the production numbers pass the magic million.

Dad has driving lessons and Mum does too and, once I am seventeen, I sit with the driving instructor, a scary experience first time round. There's an ignition switch on the dashboard to turn and there's something called a choke. There's a knack to pulling the choke out only far enough to make the car start without swamping it with petrol. If it floods it takes ten or fifteen minutes to dry out. If all else fails, there's a starting handle stored in the boot. It resembles a small T-shape crowbar inserted in a hole beneath the front bumper and cranked if the car won't start, common on cold mornings or if the battery is flat.

Dad learns how to 'double-de-clutch' so he can go down two gears in one go. An orange arrow pops out of the door to indicate turning left or right but these are difficult to see so we have to use hand signals as well – a circular anticlockwise movement for turning left, an up and down motion for slowing down and he points his arm out if he is turning right.

Dad passes his test first time but I need two attempts and pass just after my nineteenth birthday. I shake so much at the start of the second test my left foot jerks causing the car to lurch. The examiner is kind and tells me to park at the side of the road, after which he asks if I have settled down and lost my nerves. I nod.

'Now we'll start the test.'

My mother suffers similar nerves and gives up learning after three attempts.

April 1962

Gill and I spend the Easter holidays at the swimming pool. It's a hot spring and the unheated pool doesn't bother us. I've sensed some interest from a lad at the youth club and he and some of his friends come to chat to us over the fence. He's in the RAF and my parents aren't pleased as they don't want me to be a service wife. Interestingly, my mother named me Dinah after a biblical character. I hated it as people called me various versions including Diane, Diana or Deena and would often comment that Dinah was a weird name. My mother did not like shortened names but I hated having to correct people. When I met this boyfriend age 16 (he of the RAF), he called me Di. It made my mother cross but I didn't care. It was like being set free and I have been Di ever since. As for a boyfriend in the RAF, well I think travelling would be lovely but they think I could do better.

Anyway, on another day at the pool, this same guy comes up to the fence and he and his friends 'chat us up'. It's the start of my first boy/girl relationship. I'm not sure it's what

I'm dreaming of but there is something I like. Before long he asks me out. After all I am sixteen!

I can't for the life of me remember the film we went to see but I'm sure it was good.

August 1962

The O level results come by post. The phone rings and it's my friend's mother wanting to compare results. I'm still in bed, my mum having brought the results envelope up with my cup of tea. I've done well but failed Geography.

But I'm tempted to agree. In later years, returning to college to teach felt like coming home after a long holiday.

But Further Education is not on my list, my original aim Teacher Training College to qualify to teach seven-year-olds. Some of my cousins entered teaching on a two-year course at college. My goals stall when the course structure changes and, that year, teacher training is *extended to three years*, an eternity to a seventeen-year-old with a serious boyfriend. Only rich girls have cars and keeping a relationship is difficult if you leave your home town. For all my outward brashness, I am less confident than I appear. I expected I'd go to college the September I was eighteen but when I learn I can't begin my course until the following September, aged nineteen, I lose interest.

There is no other option but stay at school. Night school, day release or factory jobs are out of the question for me with my grammar school education. I look in the paper at the 4-5 pages of jobs. Mum says there's plenty of work for those who want it. Crèches and nurseries are opening for mothers. Some of my friends go shelf filling in the evenings. One shelf filling job had over two hundred applications from women who previously did war work. Mum tries working at a local pyjama factory called Sussman's along with women from our road but she has poor health following scarlet fever as a child. She's prone to sick headaches later known as migraines and is constantly stressed with my sister who has now left school and is not settling in well to the hearing world and a work environment. She leaves the pyjama factory eventually.

'Years ago, no-one worked after marriage,' says Mum.

That changed in the war when women were suddenly needed in the workplace. The government made it easy for women to work. They opened crèches and nurseries so women could leave their children while on the production lines.

I therefore return to the sixth form half-hearted, confused, not having considered any other career and find my passage temporarily blocked. The Head of English, annoyed at my grade 5 English Language result, grudgingly lets me study English A level. Furthermore, we have a stern and rather boring male teacher for history and economics (my first male teacher ever). I am soon not enjoying sixth form. First, my best friend, Gill, has left school and started on a secretarial course. Also, I don't share free periods with my other five gang members. I feel adrift.

Having reluctantly divulged my antipathy to the sixth form to my parents, imagine my relief when this is sympathetically embraced. Within twenty-four hours my mother has obtained an interview for me at St Albans College of Further Education. On arrival I'm shown into the office of the Head of the Secretarial Department and, as the interview develops, I mention my thwarted teaching career.

What happens next changes my life forever.

'Of course you can still do that. Do well on this course and you can teach secretarial subjects in Further Education.' I am immediately engaged. My secretarial tutor, Enid Lyall, arriving in the interview room also provides a pivotal moment in my life by agreeing I could eventually become a secretarial tutor like her although, with the term into its sixth week, her words ring in my ears.

'You'll have to work hard to catch up with the others.'

I don't care. Fortunately for me, some students have not grasped the shorthand and a remedial group has been set up plus extra work to do at home. I can join that which I do, eventually taking the end of year prize for the Secretarial B Group.

I never forget Enid Lyall's words and in 1975 I attend Welwyn Garden City Further Education College to train as a typewriting teacher. I start teaching evening classes, day release classes and move into teaching on the mainstream full-time courses within a couple of years. I attend High Wycombe College to do the Teacher's Certificate in Office Practice and by 1977 I am working on part-time contracts my hours burgeoning as I become more enthused. A full-time post is just around the corner.

That afternoon, after the interview, I go back to school to say my goodbyes. I am over school leaving age but am sent to the headmistress to explain why I'm leaving. I've been in the top five of the year for many subjects at O level and she's clearly displeased to see a promising student leave. She stands up stiffly. I tentatively hold out my hand but she declines. I visit other classrooms to say goodbye to teachers. One is encouraging.

'If it doesn't work out, you know, Miss Dwyer will always take you back.' Somehow I doubt that will happen.

Gill is already on a secretarial course at the college. There are three one-year intensive groups. They are Sec A, Sec B and Sec C – the latter raising much mirth and laughter. I am in Sec B as I've passed English O level. Gill needs to retake English so she's in Sec C. I start the next Monday, five weeks into the term.

However, within days (it seems) of starting at the college the whole world is gripped in the horror of a possible third world war when on 22 October 1962, John F Kennedy, the American President, announces Russian missile bases are established in Cuba within range of the USA.

One of our Commerce lessons ends up in a free discussion about the incident, refreshing and stimulating after constrained lesson structures at grammar school. Twenty seventeen-year-olds talk of little else. A frisson of fear ripples through the secretarial groups like an incoming tide. I wonder how it will affect my boyfriend in the RAF who could be sent anywhere in an emergency. We all breathe a sigh of relief when, on 28th October, the Cuban Crisis is deemed over.

On 2nd November, President Kennedy announces all missile bases in Cuba destroyed. The USA's blockade on Cuba is lifted on the twentieth of the month. Finally on 26th November, the US agrees to remove their missile bases from Turkey. Nine months later Kennedy and Khrushchev sign an agreement to ban nuclear testing.

Meanwhile, back in 1962, Mary Simpson is in my shorthand group as is her friend from school, Rose. I already know Mary from visits to Redbourn Youth Club. She's also a regular bell ringer, keeping this interest up through life. So I go around with Mary and Rose and we make a foursome with a girl called Jackie

Intensive doesn't go anywhere near to describing our course. The hours are 9am – 5pm five days a week with a Wednesday evening twilight class from 6pm-7.30pm. We study Law for RSA Stage I, Commerce and Accounts O level, RSA Stage I Office Practice and RSA Secretarial Duties Stage II. I take Stage III in typewriting and also pass 120 words per minute shorthand. Such courses disappear in the 70s and 80s with cuts to costs and thereby teaching hours. Dumbing down some may call it. It's the start of a drop in standards seen in vocational education and a short-sighted approach to training Britain's youngsters.

Today's students would be horrified at the lengthy hours we spent in college but also they'd be aghast at the old-fashioned methods and equipment. Of course, we didn't know better and thought it all good. We learn to type on manual typewriters and use the carriage return lever to start a new line. We relish every moment. Every Friday afternoon we type repetitive drills to music. For written subjects we make notes or copy notes from the board into exercise books. There are no handouts and the only anticipated step in new technology is the possibility of electric typewriters. I work every evening at shorthand, writing lines and lines of thick and thin strokes of Pitman New Era Shorthand. A year later and I have a fistful of qualifications which I attribute to Mrs Lyall's excellent teaching. She is my forever role model. I never forget her teaching methods, inspiration and motivation. (NB in the late 1970s, with my three daughters in school, I begin teaching secretarial students).

Towards the end of my course I'm interviewed and appointed as a Medical Secretary at Luton and Dunstable Hospital starting the end of August, after I return from holiday in France. I work with another Medical Secretary in the X-ray department. The doctor I work for is new and I discover my appointment is to enhance his status and not to do with the amount of work.

We type reports on manual Olympia typewriters and mistakes have to be rubbed out with an eraser on both top and carbon copy. Tippex is yet to appear. I make mistakes galore, my mind often elsewhere. But I don't care as by now all I want to do is get married!

Sometime in 1963, the phone rings and it's my grandmother saying she has fallen from the stepladder down the stairs. She's badly bruised and shocked. My mother is cross she didn't wait for my father to do the painting at the top of the stairs but typically, my granny did it herself. My mother visits her. Her left side including her breast is badly bruised.

Some six to twelve months later, she discovers a lump in her breast and the diagnosis is cancer so, three days after seeing the consultant, she has a mastectomy. In 1962 doctors didn't do anything lesser than full breast removal. My mother takes her to hospital and my grandmother gives instructions about what to do with her personal effects if she doesn't come through the operation. This upsets my mother and she's clearly worried. We're allowed to visit the day after the operation. I hurry home from college to accompany my mother. We take some flowers and chocolates and wait in trepidation outside the ward. In 1963 this is a major operation and we know no-one who has experienced similar. We expect a frail seventy-three-year-old lady lying weak in her bed.

What we see is anything but. As we enter St Peter's ward we spy her halfway down on the right-hand side, sitting up in bed, waving 'hurry up' as she has much to tell us. Her white soft hair is immaculate already with hair pins in place and she's a good colour mostly from her make-up.

Mum and I are visibly shocked at her bright state. No sooner have we handed her the flowers than she calls a nurse and gives her orders.

'Put them in water quickly!' She's so bossy.

My mother nudges me. We're dissolving into giggles.

'Not much wrong with her,' mutters Mum under her breath.

Granny demands all the family news and how I'm doing at school. After one hour, exhausted, we're relieved to wave goodbye. We laugh all the way home on the bus.

She is kept in hospital for about eight days and then sent to Northwood Hospital for radiotherapy treatment.

She's kept there for six weeks and has two radio-therapy treatments a week. I travel by bus to visit her one Saturday, changing buses for Northwood. I am confident travelling by bus as we often visit Rickmansworth relatives.

I sit with my grandmother for one or two hours and, although she makes little fuss, it's clear she's very sore from the treatment and the red, raw skin is visible at her neckline. My grandmother, in true Tuffin vein, makes a full recovery with no return of the cancer. She suffers no further major illness in her life which extends to eighty-seven years. She lives to enjoy my wedding and is fortunate to see three great-grandchildren.

Eventually I stop working in Dad's shop and leave Luton and Dunstable Hospital to work at St Albans City Hospital, a shorter bus ride. Here, the most common X-ray is a straightforward plate and a lateral view if necessary, often of the chest or stomach. Some patients have barium enemas or barium meals and, for those with kidney problems there's the IVP (the intravenous pyelogram) where dye is injected into the patient and X-rays are taken periodically after specified times such as five minutes, fifteen minutes and even later to see how the fluids are processed by the kidneys and evacuated from the bladder.

During my eighteen months there, technology advances. Some procedures begin to be viewed on a television screen. Change is on its way but for now there are no ultrasounds, MRI scans or other modern investigative techniques.

Holidays, Hobbies, Treats and Trips

Every year the Highland Games in Rothamsted Park take place. According to the *St Albans and Harpenden Review*, The St Albans and Mid-Herts Caledonian Society organised the first of these on June 22, 1946 at Beech Hyde Farm, Wheathampstead, initially a fundraising event to assist Scottish engineers working in aircraft factories including de Havilland in Hatfield during the Second World War who, when the war ended, were out of work. The games relocated to Clarence Park, St Albans in 1949, then moved to Rothamsted Park in 1950 continuing until its demise in the late 1950s. Happily, in 1997, the Highland Gathering was re-established at Rothamsted Park by the Harpenden Lions Club. It's now one of the largest Gatherings outside Scotland, raising tens of thousands of pounds for charity every year.

Mum and I edge closer to the cordoned off arena. Men play the bagpipes marching down the Harpenden Road and I am amused they wear skirts.

The school holidays are bliss. As a child, I sail my toy boats, made from scraps of wood, in an old tin bath. Dad collects the rainwater in the bath to fill watering cans. Hoses are yet to be popular. Some neighbours have water butts to collect rainwater. We think we're modern when we have a short piece of hose fixed to the kitchen tap to fill the tin bath via the kitchen window. During summer holidays, my sister and I play in the tent on the back lawn and, after lunch, we cycle to Batford to go swimming at Kimpton outdoor swimming pool. On wet days we take the bus to St Albans and swim at Cottonmill indoor swimming pool just off Holywell Hill. But, the favourite has to be the outdoor pool at London Colney where there is grass and a cafe. We head there during the summers when we don't go on holiday to a seaside guesthouse. London Colney is one of our day trips on a hot day.

If we are not going out I roller skate round the house. Some days we cycle to see our grandparents in Batford. A favourite is to cycle across the field paths off Cross Lane to Nomansland Common where we can run along paths and get lost before having the picnic Mum's prepared. We take a cricket set so we can play a game and, if it's a Sunday, we might watch the local cricket teams playing for real. On the common, there's a cricket pavilion with the cricket square similar to the one on Harpenden Common. The bowling area (square) is taped off to save the turf from walkers and children playing.

Dad is never more popular than when we picnic as a family. His bicycle is laden with a primus stove (a burner which uses methylated spirits) and, strapped to the rear pannier, is a small cardboard brewing-up box which contains a small teapot and two or three cups, jars of loose tea, milk and sugar lumps. While we play hide and seek, he sits waiting patiently for the kettle to boil. When the tea has brewed it's poured into cups while we eat sandwiches. Years later, as a car owner, he and my mother start travelling round the country stopping in the occasional layby to brew up on the same primus stove. Service areas are not seen, simply a small garage with two or three pumps with no shop. We've yet to hear of the word latte!

Most outings are on the 321 bus either toward St Albans direction or the opposite way towards Luton when we stop at the George. The next stop is the Embassy Cinema – a frequent alighting point for us. The three of us are always out and about in the holidays and Mum has her own way of managing her household tasks. We rarely go out on a Monday as it is wash day. Also Wednesday is when Granny visits although she often comes on outings especially to visit family.

On other days we're not restricted by household jobs. Mum's a master at dumping the breakfast washing up in the sink and leaving the house forgetting it completely.

'Up early, Rene?' Our neighbour is out putting washing on the line. There's a smell of boiling soapsuds

'We're off out. Left the dishes in the sink. Have to make the most of it.'

The chore is forgotten until we head home and turn the corner into Grove Avenue.

'Easy to do while I cook tea.'

However, often this task is delegated.

'No need to sit down.'

We've fallen through the door after an afternoon of long walks and swimming.

'What did your last servant die of?' A tea towel is thrown at us to emphasise the fact. We're made to do the washing up from when we can reach the sink and Mum's not averse to giving us the odd duster or the Ewbank sweeper.

The significance of abandoning chores became apparent years later. Daily tasks took low priority in Mum's world and getting out, encouraging us in many activities was high on her list. We were fortunate that, when we were young, she didn't work as we saw peers having to stay with grandparents in the holidays. Working is an eternal dilemma faced by mothers but, her time was the greatest gift she gave us.

Trips to Rothamsted Park are high on the agenda. We play tennis and go into the playground on the roundabouts, slides and swings. Tennis was not my strong point, so my sister prefers to play with my mother. She excels at all sports and my mother could give her a good game. We cycle across the Common and pay for a tennis court at the Lodge near the main gates. Susan and I had clips on our bikes to hold our tennis racquets.

I'm always ball girl waiting for someone to play with me. When I get my chance to play I'm easily bored and repeatedly miss the ball. I fume when my sister laughs at me although my mother's more tactful. After I join Elliswick Lawn Tennis Club with Mary Barnes, I become a fair player despite never winning matches and tournaments.

A steamy hot day sees us walking to the Common via Cravells Road. At the top of the road, the Common extends as far as the eye of a seven-year-old can see, an endless green sea of grass waving in the wind. This road was so named in the late 1800s when the first gravel was put on a road. Local children rushed to see the sight that was the new 'gravelled road' and so the name stuck. Wherever we go we first walk or cycle along Grove Road, from Grove Avenue to South Harpenden Shops.

As children, we holidayed for a week in a guest house every other year. It took place in August and we travelled for hours by train, first up to London, St Pancras, and then across London on the Underground to a mainline station serving the south coast. Often my mother sent a trunk of clothes to the hotel the week before we left home so she did not have to carry a large case.

Our first holiday after the war was Hastings in 1947 where the beaches were still covered in wire used for our defence during WW2. One of the hottest summers on record, we spent every afternoon in the local park under trees. My six-year-old sister is dark-haired, her skin rarely burning in the sun and she turns brown within days while I'm fairer, my skin burning. I hated the sand between my toes, grizzling all the time. Apparently I made everyone's holiday miserable.

Soon after that blistering heatwave, autumn set in with the trees on the Common turning a glorious golden brown. Then as winter arrived with a gust of bitter wind, we had news that at London Zoo a baby polar bear had been born, named Brumus. At the first opportunity we go to see him, first collecting my sister from Victoria station for the Christmas holiday. Crowds swarmed around the polar bear enclosure and Mum held me up so I could see this lovely white ball of fluff.

Our next holiday – I was four – was at Broadstairs and later guest house stays included Westgate and Bognor

Regis. The furthest west we travelled was Bournemouth when, on one day, we took a bus to Sandbanks and Shell Bay, a day trip forever etched on my memory when, years later, I move to Swanage and use the Sandbanks ferry on a daily basis to get to work and to visit grandchildren.

For my auburn-haired mother, sunny weather heralded extreme discomfort and in Sandown with its better climate and higher temperatures, drastic action was needed. Every year she investigated the most effective cream available on the market. Finally, she bought a wide-brimmed hat, several long sleeved T-shirts, ever longer skirts and lightweight trousers.

Holiday bookings were Saturday to Saturday. My father worked on Saturday mornings so we travelled on ahead and Dad would follow, meeting up with us at a pre-arranged point on the beach.

Every day of our holiday we head for the beach and sit on four deckchairs. Travelling light by train meant few people had their own chairs and business was brisk for deckchair attendants. At about 11am and again at 3pm, my father goes to a kiosk and fetches a tray of tea with stainless steel teapot, milk jug and sugar bowl. Tea was poured into china cups.

Guest houses provided bed, breakfast and evening meal with some offering full board. Most people had two weeks' holiday a year but my dad only had one week as there was no holiday pay at the time. We took full board one year but my parents disliked the disruption with the lunchtime wash and brush up and change of clothes and my sister and I objected to abandoning carefully crafted sandcastles. So we returned to half board with all day on the beach.

Evenings were spent walking along the promenade or, if wet, in an amusement arcade although those visits were strictly rationed by my mother. Treats were spread out over the week with the candyfloss evening a favourite. One mouthful dissolving into an empty chasm of nothingness and feverish pulling of strips which dissolved on to sticky sugary hands. Another treat was a bowl of whelks, my parents enjoying mussels or winkles and, of course, the sticky, gooey toffee apple. Our last stop would be a milk bar or café when we were treated to a hot drink of Horlicks before we returned to the guest house and bed.

Our photo album shows year on year of holidays with boats built in the sand, Jokari played on the beach and sitting on the water's edge. My reluctance to enter the sea or brave the depths and learn to swim was frequently mentioned at family gatherings.

Every other year we stayed at home and went on day trips by bus or steam train. One year, we went to Brighton by train and to Hampton Court, Kew Gardens, London and Whipsnade Zoo. One day we went to London Colney swimming pool where we could sit on grass between swims and eat our picnic. Soon after my eleventh birthday, with more income from the shop business, we went away every year.

One favourite occupation when travelling by train were the I-Spy books. The I-Spy club run by retired headmaster, Charles Ward, known as Big Chief I-Spy, boasted half a million members and was hugely popular. The books from W H Smith or newsagents could be bought with pocket money. Some examples were *I-Spy at the Seaside* and *I-Spy on the Train*. If we spotted something, we wrote down where we saw it and the date. Once completed, the book was sent away for an I-Spy badge.

School holidays included at least one shopping trip. When shopping in St Albans, Mum and I always go for coffee in little Thrales cake shop and café in French Row and, if out with my grandmother and sister, we enjoy a treat in the Barn Restaurant on St Peter's Street, opposite Mark's and Spencer's. We're told to mind our p's and q's – a phrase derived from the words please and thank you.

In London, we eat in Lyons Corner House. Eating out is not common in the fifties but my parents now have more money and Saturday lunchtimes see them in Mary Ellen's, later The Inn on the Green.

More Italians lived in Britain in the post-war years, as many had been prisoners of war and stayed on in the UK, especially if they met and married an English girl. In 1955 Italians, Frank and Aldo Berni, founded a steak chain which contributed to the growth of dining out by working class families. The Tudor Tavern, in French Row, St Albans, was a Berni we visited with boyfriends. The standard choice was prawn cocktail followed by steak, chips and peas, with Black Forest gateau for dessert. There was a Berni Inn at The Three Hammers at Chiswell Green, St Albans where I celebrated my twenty-first birthday with Graham and his parents.

I eat at Mary Ellen's with my parents but, those days, there were only couples as families with children didn't eat out. Also there were no all-female tables. Girls' nights out were unheard of. Few women earned money or chose how family income was spent.

One half-term holiday Mum asked me if I'd like to try the launderette for fun as one had opened in Station Road. What a novelty! The first UK launderette, fully automated, coin operated and unmanned had opened on 9th May 1949 in Queensway, London. Later some launderettes did have an attendant and one could leave washing for a small fee. There was an attendant at our launderette but customers had to operate the machines themselves. It was exciting, therefore, to try out this new phenomenon. As we have a car, Dad takes the bags of washing to his shop in the morning. My mother and I later take the bags up Station Road and we had many giggles about getting the soap powder out of the machine and putting the money in the slot.

The first time the machine spun the clothes, my mother screamed.

'Oo er where's it gone!'

'There it is.' The machine was slowing by now.

We sighed with relief when it stopped and we could see it again. We checked everything thoroughly when it came out of the machine as we expected the clothes to be damaged.

My mother was amazed at how easy her washday had been; she was so pleased at the result that, before long, this trip became a regular weekly jaunt. Every Monday, my father took the washing, stuffed in bags and placed on the back seat of his little Morris Minor, to Harpenden Village and carried them from the car to his shop. Soon after this, my mother would cycle from Grove Avenue to Harpenden to work, serving customers from about 10am on the counter, leaving her bike in the rear back room. After lunch with my dad in Granny's flat above the shop, Mum would take the washing to the launderette, go shopping while the programme was running, return to take it from the washing machine and put it in the tumble dryer, then return it to Dad's car. Sometimes, when Dad was short of staff, she helped on the counter until about 4.30pm. She loved being back behind a shop counter. Usually she was home before I arrived from school but occasionally our homecomings coincided and we walked up Grove Avenue together. These were golden times when we enjoyed one another's company.

Holidays and French Exchange

By 1962, some of my more affluent school mates go on package holidays abroad, pioneered by Vladimir Raitz, the co-founder of the Horizon Holiday Group. When I mention foreign holidays Mum is dismissive.

'I can't see the point of going to a hot country.'

'Why?'

'I can't sit in the sun because of my red hair and sensitive skin.'

Mum has other reasons.

'I don't like the heat and wouldn't like the food.'

Also she didn't want to fly.

We had never been abroad. Some girls at grammar school had been overseas and the Swedish twins in my year flew back and forth each year to Sweden to see their father. Package holidays were still unusual for the likes of us but my parents want me to have opportunities. The ski trip was one. My sister, Susan, had been to Jersey with the Guides travelling by ferry and she had also been to Le Touquet in France similarly with the Guides. However, I missed out on such trips because as I only stayed in the Brownies three weeks, I never became a fully enrolled Brownie let alone a Girl Guide.

1962

This year my penfriend, Michelle Dupeu, stayed with me for three weeks. She looked down on my family and was visibly irritated when I went out one evening with Graham.

Michelle had been told it rained in England and it was always cold. While I'm photographed in a blouse and skirt, she felt cold. Within days, a parcel arrived from France containing warm jumpers. My mother noticed Michelle's clothes were expensive unlike mine which were mainly home-sewn by me.

She was horrified my father was a shoe repairer which hurt me deeply as my father was a real gentleman. In France, she said, they were low class whereas my father owned his own business, employed staff and also later owned the property where they all worked. I was glad when she went home. Especially as she told my mother that, in France, men who went into the RAF like Graham only did that if they were no good for anything else. Graham had undertaken an apprenticeship at RAF Halton which was highly regarded.

She was included when we met up with my large youth club group. However, none of the boys made any attempt to be friendly as they were mainly from the local secondary school and, subsequently, hadn't learnt French. Also Michelle was aloof and they found it difficult to converse with her.

After my secretarial examinations the following year, I go on an exchange holiday to her home. She lived at a hotel her parents owned in La Ferte Mace, Orne, Normandy – The Hotel du Grand Turc. I was to discover her father was a brilliant chef.

I was the first person in our family to fly on an aeroplane. For this great event, my parents, grandmother and sister came up to London airport and stood on the roof of the terminal to wave me goodbye. Of course, I couldn't see them. My mother told me she had a lump in her throat as the plane took off and quickly looked small in the sky and she couldn't believe her little girl was in the sky. I was not nervous as, like all young people, the implications of one's actions and travels are not a consideration. However, other than my school trip to Derbyshire, a week skiing and three days in hospital for a tonsillectomy at the age of seven, I'd never been away and I was homesick before the plane was in the air.

At Orly airport Michelle met me on her own. I thought this strange but she guided us away from the airport and after a long walk and rides on the Metro, with my case, we ended up in an apartment building. The flat was owned by her aunt and the proximity to the centre of Paris enabled her to show me the sights of Paris. Michelle also had another aunt in Rambouillet and after three days in Paris, we travelled there, staying two days, near to Rambouillet and Versailles. On reflection they did me proud on my visit and I appreciated it despite my homesickness. I understood enough French to know her aunt told her off for being rude to me. Her cousin was nicer.

I have photos of Michelle, her cousin and myself in the vast grounds of Rambouillet. I am wearing a shift dress, fashionable in 1963. I also sported some court shoes with a medium size stiletto heel. Burgundy and black, I thought they were the best. Comfortable or not, I wore them throughout my stay in France.

It was August 1963 and a few weeks before I started work at Luton and Dunstable Hospital as a medical secretary. Therefore, I only stay in France for two weeks as I also miss my boyfriend, Graham, and feel homesick for other members of my family. This was surprising as I always envied my sister her absences at boarding school.

On this, my return visit, I saw her in her home environment, a good quality hotel. We ate in the restaurant with the other hotel guests who knew Michelle was the owner's daughter and also I was *la petite Anglaise.*

I was not comfortable staying there as her parents decided the easiest way to accommodate *la petite Anglaise* was in a twin-bedded hotel room. So we became hotel guests for two weeks. I had never before stayed in a posh hotel. In the restaurant we were served by her parents' staff. I was taken aback at how rudely Michelle spoke to them something I found embarrassing. She had obviously decided the previous year, I was beneath her, she saw me as an inconvenience she was keen to get rid of, whereas I'd tried hard with her and my mother particularly went out of her way to be accommodating.

But her parents were friendly to me and made me welcome. Each day her father pushed a wad of francs into Michelle's hand for spending money. She admitted her parents were too busy to spend time with her something I found sad.

One night Michelle and I were in our hotel bedroom and I used a depilatory cream. She said this was unheard of in France and girls always showed masses of underarm hair.

'Why can't you stay for three weeks?' Michelle's parents persistently ask for me to stay longer but I make the excuse I need to go back to prepare for starting work. My secretarial course completed, I'm due to start at Luton and Dunstable Hospital at the end of August. Truth was, despite the lovely hotel food, I didn't want to stay any longer.

Back home and the French food is a memory. My mother rarely cooks cakes other than rock cakes. Sometimes I think her brain is stuck in the days of rationing and fears of shortages but she does have knowledge and skill. One Sunday she makes a Victoria sandwich cake for tea and the whole family, including Granny and Susan, is so excited about it and cannot wait for tea-time. We eat it with relish making ecstatic noises so she apologises for not giving us such treats more often.

Secretly, I think Mum would have liked a career. She was more suited to working in my father's shop than being a stay-at-home housewife. While she sang and cleaned, rolled sheets in the mangle and took pride in her Baby Burco boiler with its whiter than white results, she clearly hankered for more. After I married and left home she started a secretarial course tutored by my role model, Enid Lyall.

However, my parents did exercise their intellect with new television programmes. They love *Quatermass* and Dad likes *Sportsview* with Peter Dimmock and, at last, my parents accept I'm old enough to stay up and watch TV with them. My grandmother is still a regular visitor especially if Billy Graham is singing at Wembley on his tour of Britain.

I return from France with a stomach upset which refuses to settle. Eventually, a worse bug hit me in November diagnosed as gastroenteritis. I'm in bed recovering from this when my mother comes upstairs in a distressed state to say John F Kennedy has been shot in Dallas. The date was 22 November 1963. My mother, along with many people, hoped for a better world with this young vibrant American president but, sadly, it was not to be.

After I returned from France I began working at Luton and Dunstable Hospital as secretary to the junior radiologist, Dr Kenney. A few weeks later, I attend the College of Further Education, meeting classmates and exchanging news for the Secretarial prize-giving. My Secretarial Tutor was clearly disappointed. She had urged me the previous June to pursue a post in London because of my excellent skills.

February 1964

And so to the Beatles… This Liverpool group rose to fame in 1961 while I was studying for my O-levels. I had already taken Maths and Latin early as I was in the top sets. My mother doesn't hide her disgust at the way girls swoon and crowd the airport roof when they fly in to London. She has already shown dislike of rock and roll music too, which she believes is not music.

'It can't be a dance if the two people don't hold each other.'

I doubted she would let me go to a live concert or club so I don't ask.

In February, the Beatles record their first LP, *Please, Please Me*, and make their debut on *Thank Your Lucky Stars*. On Saturday evenings I watch pop programmes on television singing and dancing in the sitting room, my parents sitting in the kitchen diner across the hall.

The winter of 1963 brings repeated snowfalls for three months. After suffering the journey of two buses during this, one of the worst winters in history, around March 1964 I see a post advertised in the Herts advertiser for a medical secretary in the x-ray department at St Albans City Hospital. Tired of getting two buses to work, this job involves only one bus. I'm successful and begin working there in the May.

The highlight of my twenty months there is the department Christmas party. We can bring boyfriends and there is wine in abundance. The head radiologist and the junior

radiologist start to make jokes and then we're dancing to the music and before I know it we're in one of the X-ray rooms. They lift me on to one of the x-ray couches and say they're going to examine me. It's a hilarious moment never to be repeated as the head radiographer comes in and immediately tells them off.

I'm still keen to learn to cook. I'd first learnt to make simple dishes such as toast and tea at school but at nineteen, after I am engaged, I attend an evening class in Bride's Cookery. When I say I work at the City Hospital, I let slip that the geriatric ward above X-ray is noisy and the teacher says her husband is a patient there. I wish I'd held my tongue. This is my first encounter with a family of someone with dementia.

I'm keen to be the perfect wife so I practise at home. Mum still says I use too many eggs. After I'm married, I cook every day with recipes loaned from friends. I cut recipes carefully from magazines and stick them in my Personal Cookery Book. As for cooking methods, in those days, it was all boiling or roasting.

However, after enjoying steaks at Berni Inn, St Albans, Mum tries grilling!

And So To Independence

I can't wait to get married. At eighteen, despite not being able to vote until twenty-one, I feel grown-up enough for marriage. I have already ditched my A level studies on spurious grounds. Believe me, I can't wait to get to grips with rushing home from work to cook a meal, clean a house, the washing and ironing. Of course, the novelty soon wears off.

Eventually I start dating with a variety of types, most unsuitable and quickly dumped after the first date. But one does stick around long enough to draw the attention of my parents to my new found maturity. One, two, three dates, two weeks, three weeks, two months, three. This is the longest time I have stuck with a gangly youth with tobacco-stained fingers without getting bored. Mistakenly, I harbour a feeling they'll be pleased. After all, my sister is four years older than I am and she has, by now, several boys she sees on Saturdays at London deaf clubs. They also visit us at home on Sundays for tea.

I also have several friends who have boyfriends but my parents make it clear that my schoolwork must come first and I'm too young to consider 'going steady' as it is known.

So I sum up courage, tell my newest love we must resort to meeting at the local youth club and friends' houses. Communication via telephone ceases and the letters lie hidden in my underwear drawer. We doubt we will ever have my parents' approval, but obstinately carry on.

Soon, I ask my father, who can refuse me nothing, and he sorts my mother out. My boyfriend calls for me and starts taking me out.

So, having got that far, two years later, I argue for marriage. I say, I know the risks, can earn my keep, will use family planning so I don't become a teenage mother, but all to no avail.

As far as I am concerned there's nothing to stop me getting married. If others are managing marriage and a rented flat, then so can I, regardless of whether I am a teenager or not. I can sew, cook a few cake recipes and I am fast completing a knitted cardigan for my fiancé at the time, which is unfortunately going horribly wrong, reminiscent of my fateful knitting disasters in Miss F's class. The right front is decidedly longer than the left but I knit away determined to show my future mother-in-law I'm domesticated and care enough to marry her son.

'She'll never let him wear it,' says my mother.

The 'she' is my mother-in-law to be.

Of course, all my protestations are a load of baloney. In 1964 no one lived together without getting married and sex outside marriage was frowned on. The Pill is yet to arrive but, up until the Big Day, we have the best contraceptive available. Free and requiring no action on our part. Abstinence, otherwise known as 'terrified of getting pregnant'.

However, some are brave, we might say careless, and do not use our terrified method. I am surrounded by myriad acquaintances who have hastily-arranged Saturday weddings conducted at St Albans Registry Office. It's not unusual to find via my mother's sharp antennae system or over-the-counter talk that an acquaintance or relative is now married. Sometimes it's a grammar school pupil who left quietly on Friday not to return. Alternatively, some return on a Monday with a wedding ring on her finger. My mother and grandmother lower their voices and say that most terrifying of all phrases.

'They had to get married!'

'It's a shotgun wedding.' My Granny is sure.

The photographs are keenly viewed by interested – or perhaps just nosy – parties. The bride wears a loose cream dress and is holding her bouquet strategically over the beginnings of a bulge. Five to six months later she's walking the streets with a large Marmet pram bought by the grandparents who insist to friends that the baby is premature.

This I realise is what my mother is scared of. She has prided herself in excellent childrearing skills. Her girls must be more polite, more intelligent and successful than any offspring of my many cousins. Of course, my mum, an only child, has numerous cousins most of whom reside in large families, enjoying fun and laughter. Some are obsessed with education. Doing well at school, I reckon, is the only way to be allowed to go courting. I bury myself and all my angst into studying.

I try to make a friend of my mother, the obstacle to my happiness. Instead of sulking, I converse at dinner, agree to go to events and places to show I am a studious seventeen-year-old with no sex drive. I ask about her courting experience, not because I don't know the details but because I do. She started going out with my dad at sixteen but seems to have forgotten. I jiggle memories and make noises of appreciation that she met my father at all. This is when the big secret comes out.

The age of twenty is a magic age, I discover.

'Then, no-one can say you are a teenage bride.'

So I was right after all. She's terrified I'll be one of those girls queuing outside St Albans registry office on a Saturday.

1964

It's September and by now things have calmed down. A holiday in Sheringham in June was amazingly condoned by my parents. Graham and I plan to get engaged on my nineteenth birthday. He takes me to see *Round the Horn* on the London stage, a treat that thrills. My mother realises she's never taken me to a London theatre. Any outings have to be good for my deaf sister so musicals or pantomimes are out. Mum asks if I would like to go to *My Fair Lady* with my parents alone, not exactly my idea of fun. The show has been running since 1958 and we're six years on.

Graham and I have our photograph taken by Juliet Haddon in Harpenden and it's published in the local newspaper. At the time I have a new hairstyle, a bun on the top of my head. I use Kirby grips and pins to fix the shape. It's called the Beehive, the name coming from its shape. Girls backcomb their hair until it stands vertically while many adults wonder what is happening underneath.

Eva, Graham's mum, is homely and loving and I adore her. She makes me welcome. It's a wonderful lasting relationship which survives my later separation from her son. She confides in me that Graham going into the

RAF broke her heart. She worried people would wonder why he wanted to leave home. Then, most young people lived at home until they married. Few went to college or university. Graham had joined other apprentices (the 96th entry) at RAF Halton. Trenchard's Brats was the nickname for all apprentices between 1922, when the scheme started, and 1993 when it ceased. The sculpture at RAF Halton represents the brass cube, a test job undertaken during technical training and the Wheel Badge worn proudly by generations of the Brats.

On my nineteenth birthday, feeling grand, I wear a new coat and proudly hold out my left hand to reveal my engagement ring. We venture by train to the West End and plan to marry in May 1966.

I am working and begin spending my small salary on bottom drawer items. Graham and I go window shopping. I buy an eiderdown and a candlewick bedspread, both in lemon. Secretly, I buy sexy lingerie and hide it beneath the tea towels Mum has given me.

Now it's all change. Far from resisting the idea of a blessed union between the two of us, my parents seem keen to take on the mood of the moment. It's a far cry from the day when my fiancé sat in our dining room trembling as he asked if we could marry. That evening, my parents, politely non-judgemental, fired questions in quick succession. They visibly relaxed when we said we wished to marry in eighteen months' time – only four months before my twenty-first birthday. The lack of urgency was apparently comforting.

However, the mood changes when my uniformed RAF recruit is given orders for an accompanied overseas posting in December 1965. Suddenly we don't want to wait until May 1966 but feel the need to marry as soon as possible – September 1965 if it's feasible – and the date leaps forward eight months. My mother, having initially showed some reluctance at the earlier date, leaps out of bed the next day and starts a book which documents everything to do with our special day. It's a large exercise book and is labelled

Operation Wedding 1965

The time set is noon at St John's with a small reception in St Albans. St Michael's Manor Hotel in Fishpool Street is selected for our fifty guests. My grandmother, having suffered the disappointments of her daughter's hasty wedding preparations in 1939, bears a broad smile for the whole eight months enjoying every minute.

Frenzied preparations begin. My mother fires off a torrent of new ideas daily, flooding every conversation. The eyes of aunts and uncles glaze over when they meet on the street. The phone is permanently in use, friends and relatives are invited round for brain picking. We embark on safari type shopping expeditions sometimes simply to buy an artificial rose or Mum's hat, Granny's shoes or my sister's dress material. These treks require a drive to Watford in Dad's Morris Minor. As a novice, my driving is punctuated by gurgling screams from my mother as we filter at newly-formed junctions – one-way systems are new. White lines on tarmac are apparently more stressful than bobbing along on the 321 bus. For Mum every junction heralds a crash.

Halfway through 1965, Graham's cousin gets married and the day is dissected, photos scrutinised and anecdotes recounted. Mum consults other relatives about myriad issues.

April showers, May sunshine. 1965 marches on. The heat is now on. The dress! White? Of course. I am adamant. I haven't lost my virginity yet and should last out for the next four months. What am I doing about my special dress? Tessa, a girl I work with has her dress made by a wedding dress hire company, relinquishing it on the Monday, all for the princely price of £10. Initially, dismissive of the dress hire route, Mum, seeing the wonderful result, dutifully returns it after which it's hired out for £5 a time on several more occasions.

In the weeks and months preceding our special day, Graham and I disappear of an evening for a drive. Our first stop is the pub but we can't admit that as Mum views public houses as common. So we call it a drive. She must realise we don't drive further than Nomansland Common to park and steam up the windows.

One balmy evening, light tapping on the window sends my heart racing.

Winding the window down – the winder only works if you are lucky – we come face to face with the old style bobby – the one with the shaped helmet.

'Hello, hello, hello what's going on here?' He asks if we have seen a black Austin 7 car with a couple in it. Of course, we haven't seen anything other than each other's body parts for two hours and I dare say the other courting couples in Austin 7s would say the same. Later, when our legs stop trembling and we recover our breath, we wonder if he is a voyeur posing as a copper.

With stomachs knotted, we worry for weeks that we have been reported and harbour a dread of a burley copper's knock on the door. But frightened into giving our names and addresses to the guy in uniform, we wonder whether news will get back. I jump out of my skin every time the phone rings. Has someone told my mother? The worst could happen. She might even cancel our wedding. In hindsight, of course, she wouldn't. It would have been too embarrassing. We hear no more and don't venture to Nomansland again.

I want a small wedding. The idea of a guest list of two hundred does not appeal – I doubt I'll enjoy it, more likely die of embarrassment and worry about hitches. Fifty should do – just close relatives. If I extend it to all the Tuffins, Munts, Westons and Smiths, we will end up with about five hundred.

Anyway, come September 1965, I manage to get up the aisle still a virgin and after a dodgy, heart-sink moment when the vicar calls my husband-to-be, to Brian – the name of my friend's husband – a couple he married a few weeks before – we find ourselves husband and wife.

Another slight hitch comes to light a few weeks later when watching our wedding cine film shot by a well-meaning acquaintance. We are treated at length to the sight of the church choir members arriving in casual clothes while the bona-fide exquisitely-dressed invited guests are ignored by the wannabe cameraman and barely appear. We laugh every time the film is shown.

To ensure we get to our wedding night destination

on the same evening, Graham works non-stop on his Hillman Imp for two weeks. Our Exodus is finalised by heading westwards to our honeymoon hotel in Devon, arriving after 11pm exhausted. But not so exhausted that we can't do what we have married for.

While some of our youth club friends take planes to far off lavish hotspots only recently available to the masses, we honeymoon modestly at Goodrington Sands near Paignton. The hotel earns its September keep with coach parties of grey-haired pensioners in ex-RAF blazers, ladies in twinsets and blue-rinse hair styles, all of whom seem rather old to us. We are viewed with amusement as their holiday novelty to write home about. One night we are asked outright if we are honeymooners, after which we become the subject of their scrutiny, sly smiles and well-meaning advice.

So keen are we to begin our life as the average Mr and Mrs Ordinary, we cut short the honeymoon by four days, to rush back to our Wiltshire love nest and undertake exciting tasks such as cooking burnt breakfast, washing up, shopping and making bad pastry. We live on the first floor of an old lady's house and share a bathroom with anonymous residents on the second floor who frequently take all the hot water and leave shaving stubble and worse around the basin.

Well I think they are anonymous until one year later, on moving to a self-contained caravan by the Thames, I discover the owner of the stubble and pubic hairs has followed me to Lechlade.

Epilogue

Sadly for us, our anticipated overseas posting was changed to unaccompanied, something that disappointed us both and, after a tearful farewell on a London station, I returned to Harpenden to live with my parents for the year he was away. I worked in St Albans for an estate agent which provided me with the experience I needed for later homeownership. Living back with my parents also enabled me to save up for the essential deposit.

My new husband stored his leave due from his year in Bahrain, using it in September 1966 to fly home for a month, during which time I had my 21st birthday celebration. I amused myself while he was away by planning this extended holiday, starting with a few days in Virginia Water, close to Heathrow where he was to land. Whereas his departure for Bahrain the previous December had been by RAF transport, his flight back for his UK leave was by civilian airline. During our time in Surrey, we visited some tourist attractions in Surrey including Windsor Castle. After this, we spent ten days in a caravan in Charmouth exploring nearby beaches and surrounding countryside. (Charmouth was later to become a favourite destination when we had young children). Finally, we travelled to Harpenden to spend some time with Graham's parents which allowed us to meet up with old school friends and those from the youth club. Graham's parents, Eva and Ron, took us for a celebratory meal at the Three Horseshoes Public House in St Albans for my 21st birthday.

This time, saying goodbye was easier as Graham was only left with eight weeks to serve in Bahrain before returning permanently to the UK. Once we knew where he would be posted – RAF Brize Norton – I travelled down to look for suitable accommodation. Flats and other rentals were in short supply but I found a caravan site with a large caravan available to rent. On the day he was to return, his flight – due around 1am – came into RAF Lyneham. I drove down with plenty of time to spare which was fortuitous as, at the last minute, I took a wrong turn and needed to turn round. The ditch at the side of the road wasn't visible in the mirror and the car was soon upended. I got out of the car thinking that there would be no one around to help me but, fortunately, a driver stopped and between us we shifted the car out of the ditch. Obviously puzzled as to why I was on a lonely road in the early hours of the morning, he asked me where I was going. Still in shock and barely able to speak, I pointed towards the airfield and then moved my hand to point to a solitary aircraft coming into land.

'My husband,' I stammered, 'is on that flight.'
'So… please excuse me if I rush off.'

Acknowledgements

With thanks to my cousin, Colin Munt, for providing much of the Munt family history reported here and for providing anecdotes and memories from his childhood. Also, Jill Castle for giving me access to the book she compiled at the end of Eva Castle's life (Graham's mother) so that her memories and background history could be included here. Thanks also to

Norman and Valerie Payne for their recollections of my Granddad Munt.

While this first edition does not include photographs, I am particularly indebted to Harpenden Local History Society for their help in 2012 when they scanned my family albums for their website. Also Gavin and Rosemary Ross for their help answering questions via email. The History Society provided me with a CD of all the images which related to life in Harpenden. Some more personal images I needed to photograph. The Harpenden website also provided factual information. I was lucky to visit their exhibitions in Park Hall.

Special thanks to my second cousin Peter Wilson who shared his family tree and details of relatives who lived in Queen's Road including Mollie Walters and family for telling me about Herbert Tuffin, my school friends, Gill Holdaway, Xana Mason and Christine Rice nee MacLennan, for reminding me of school events, Albert Calleweart for his extensive emails documenting much information including the shops in Southdown and providing photographs. I also explored www.genesreunited.com discovering relatives who messaged sharing family information.

The research has been fun and rewarding as only other writers can begin to comprehend. Following my letter in the *Herts Advertiser*, many people wrote or talked to me sharing memories. These are too numerous to mention individually. My good friend and colleague, Helen MacDonald, read early drafts of this book and gave valuable advice.

Finally, many thanks go to Sathnam Sanghera for his Memoir Writing Workshop at Winchester Writers' Conference/Festival 2015 and I am grateful to him for signing his book, *The Boy with the Topknot*, with a personal dedication to me and the encouraging comment *'one day you will write something better than this'*. Well I'm not too sure about that!

About the Author

Di Castle experienced a nomadic existence in Hertfordshire, Wiltshire, Oxfordshire, Middlesex, Buckinghamshire, finally settling in Swanage, Dorset for twenty-one years. She now lives in Southsea.

Red House to Exodus is a memoir by Di Castle who was born at Harpenden Memorial Hospital (known as the Red House). Set in Harpenden, it spans the 1950s and 1960s – a time of great social change following the Second World War. It includes her home experience, early schooldays – the local infant school had quite undesirable outside toilets – and the headmistress travelled by bus bringing her cocker spaniel, Andy, who slept in a basket under her desk. Subsequently, transition to grammar school was followed by secretarial training at St Albans College of Further Education. She then worked as a medical secretary at Luton and Dunstable Hospital and later at St Albans City Hospital.

The author has used research of the 1950s and 1960s to place her life in context. From starting school, Festival of Britain in 1951, the Coronation in 1953, milk and coal delivered by horse and cart, moving house, numerous pets such as rabbits, a tortoise, budgies, and even a mouse! She and her sister entertained themselves with skipping ropes, Jokari, hopscotch, a den made out of runner bean canes and hessian sacks that brought our coal for our open fire and growing flowers and vegetables in our own dedicated gardens.

References

The following are a small selection of many websites I used during my research (please note some of these may no longer be available):

- www.hertsmemories.org.uk
- www.wheathampstead.net/history
- www.genesreunited.co.uk,
- www.ancestry.co.uk,
- http://www.hertfordshire-genealogy.co.uk,
- www.mrsbeeton.com,
- http://www.whirligig-tv.co.uk/radio/
- http://news.bbc.co.uk/onthisday,
- http://www.whirligig-tv.co.uk/
- http://www.whirligig-tv.co.uk/tv/children/muffin/muffin.htm
- http://www.20thcenturylondon.org.uk
- http://www.fashion-era.com/1950s/
- Chimney Sweep information from http://www.thisisnottingham.co.uk/bygones/Bygones-Memories-chimney-sweep/article-1764111-detail/article.html

I am grateful to the following authors whose books I found helpful:

ARTHUR, Max, *Forgotten Voices of the Great War*. A new history of WW1 in the words of the men and women who were there.

COOPER, John, *A Harpenden Childhood Remembered*. Growing up in the 1940s and 1950s.

FEENEY, Paul, *A 1950s Childhood, From Tin Baths to Bread and Dripping*, History Press, 2009

FOLEY, Winifred, *A Child of the Forest*

GREY, Edwin, *Cottage Life in a Hertfordshire Village*, 1977, Harpenden and District Local History Society

GOCKELEN-KOZLOWSKI, Tom, *The Seven-Inch Single*, Telegraph Magazine 28th March 2010.

HOWARD, Michael and LOUIS, William Roger, 1998, Oxford University Press, *The Oxford History of the Twentieth Century*,

HYAMS, Jacky, *Hoop Skirts and Pony Tails*, 2016, John Blake Books

MOYNAHAN, Brian, *Looking Back at Britain, The Road to Recovery*, 1950s, Readers Digest

DK Millennium, *20th Century Day by Day*, Foreword by Jeremy Paxman

RUSSELL, Tony and BECKETT, Francis, 1956, *The Year That Changed Britain*, Biteback Publishing

SUMMERS, Julie, *Stranger in the House* (Women's stories of men returning from the Second World War)

WEBSTER, Ralph, 2007. *It started With a Green Line Bus*, The Book Castle

WOODWARD, Sue and Geoff, *The Hatfield, Luton and Dunstable Railway*

DI CASTLE, AUTHOR – BASED IN SOUTHSEA

Accredited speaker for Dorset and Hampshire WIs, Di speaks on – writing, poetry, deaf awareness and introduction to BSL.

Available for school visitsdicastlewriter.wordpress.com

- Shortlisted for the U3A short story competition 2022
- Regular attendee at Winchester Writers' events
- Winner of 2010 Retirement Competition – Winchester
- Winner 2012 Sustaining the Environment – Winchester
- Third Place in Short Story Competition Hampshire Writers Society
- Highly commended in many other competitions
- Member of Hampshire Writers' Society
- Member of Alliance of Independent authors
- Qualified Further and Higher Education tutor and Dyslexia Specialist
- BSL speaker experienced with both oral and signing deaf people.

SHOULD I WEAR FLORAL (2017) and other poems on Life, Love and Leaving. *A celebration of the last 30 years*

GRANDMA'S POETRY BOOK (2014) – *'makes you laugh, makes you cry'* Ideal Christmas or new grandparent gift. Order direct

Available in bookshops – please support independent bookshops in your area

dcastle32@talktalk.net
https://www.facebook.com/pages/Di-Castle-Writer/266866193324409
Twitter @dinahcas

Out soon – *Sharing The Silence* (two sisters, different lives)

This book is printed on paper from sustainable sources managed under the Forest Stewardship Council (FSC) scheme.

It has been printed in the UK to reduce transportation miles and their impact upon the environment.

For every new title that Troubador publishes, we plant a tree to offset CO_2, partnering with the More Trees scheme.

For more about how Troubador offsets its environmental impact, see www.troubador.co.uk/sustainability-and-community